It Happened in Florence

Nita Tucker

with Christa McDermott

ISBN: 1453774491

ISBN-13: 9781453774496

To *my guys*…

Marco, Leo and Giovanni who 'fathered' *The Florentine* and
continue to have it flourish in my absence.

Luca and Logan, my grandsons
…for whom, it was worth leaving Florence.

Tony, the love of my life,
who 'gave me' Florence and has always
made sure my dreams came true.

Table Of Contents

It Happened in Florence

Riding my bike over the Ponte Vecchio, I stop to look across at the Uffizi Gallery or the church of San Miniato on the hill overlooking Florence, and say to myself,

I live here! This is my life!

I had, at last fulfilled my long held dream to live in Europe. Florence was my life for four incredible years. Pedaling through the streets instantly and intimately connected me with the past and present of this unique city; cycling by the palazzos, churches, museums and galleries, I admired the legacy of its long-ago Renaissance, only to have my head turned by the well-heeled Florentines popping in and out of designer stores and chic café-bars.

The life I discovered in Florence fully embraced the old and the new of the city. With my husband, Tony, and our Italian partners, I set up *The Florentine*, a newspaper for ex-pats living in Florence, as well as for the many English speaking tourists who visit this beguiling city every year. I was the editor-in-chief and at the center of all the action. I reveled in the opportunity to meet so many new and captivating people; excited that they all seemed to want to meet me! Everything that was enticing in the city's history and vibrant present was waiting for me to discover and share with the readers. I had a mission, and a bike...and already more than I'd hope for.

It was usually my bicycle that transported me to the unexpected stopping points with which my life in Florence was abundant. Some days I could be seen pedaling to the office to meet my talented, confounding and gorgeous Italian business partners; or to interview politicians, designers from fashion dynasties, members of the Florentine nobility or visiting celebrities. Other times I'd throw on a black dress and saddle up to attend a special event: maybe the opening of a gallery; or a privileged sneak-peak at rarely viewed treasures in the company of distinguished patrons of the arts; or perhaps a fashion show…that I may have been officially invited to or about to crash. And, on other days, I would take a short and leisurely ride to meet my girlfriends at a piazza café or hotel roof-top bar - to talk, laugh and cry over friends, family and fashion and come up with ideas as to how we could make a difference within the Florence we loved and adored.

Every day proved an adventure; the highs were certainly high. But there were lows too, make no mistake. Saying goodbye to my husband when he returned to the US after a year, soon to be followed by my daughter Montana, was acutely painful. The trials of adjusting to this physical separation required us to re-assess our relationships and work out new (and eventually better) ways to connect, relate and share our love for each other. There were moments of real isolation, when still figuring out how I weave my way into the tightly knitted Florentine circles, I'd cry with longing for my own family and nurturing US girlfriends. On top of all this, a lack of money - to fund me and the newspaper - was a constant source of worry, requiring much juggling and negotiation. And while I was in awe of being in Italy, loving my discovery of its history, life and people, I also had to face that there were just some aspects of its culture that left me frustrated, upset and feeling far from home. Yet, those times

I stopped my bike on the Ponte Vecchio and took in the wonder of it all, I had no doubt whatsoever that the highs, certainly in number, by far exceeded the lows. It is on a circuitous, and not strictly chronological, journey through both ups and downs that this book will take you.

One of my greatest insights about living in Italy came from my friend Stephano, who once told me, in the most disparaging tone,

Americans, think the best way to get from point A to point B is a straight line.

His comment explains much about Italy - from the lack of signage on the highways to what makes Italians great lovers. Essentially, for Italians, the direct route has no appeal - it's the most *interesting* way of getting anywhere that grabs their attention. What they abhor with a passion is *boredom*. For anything to be worth their time, effort and energy - whether a journey, a task, a job - the *process* of arriving at the end goal must be challenging, fascinating and open to many interpretations with nothing fixed in black and white. Short and quick just doesn't come into it - intensely frustrating if you want to set up your internet, do some basic banking, or find the right exit on the motorway; but eye-opening, nourishing and enormously fun as a philosophy for life.

I hope each of the stopping points in this book will demonstrate the extent to which I came to embrace this Italian need to avoid the dull and boring and how I remained continually alert to the departure from the plan, the unexpected offer and the possibility of adventure.

It is the people I met in Florence, and the lives and events into which they invited me (and into which I often asked to enter), that give the twists and turns to this definitely *not* as the crow flies route. From arriving in Florence in April 2004, returning to the US four years later, each short chapter of this book is a memento of how my time in this enchanting city impacted me in ways I could never have imagined when I first arrived. Dip in, dip out, read the pieces in any order - make up your own journey.

I hope that the sum of all these memories of Florence experienced *my way*, collected here, is the bigger story of why dreams are not things to remain floating in the ether to think about only on cold and bluer days - but intimate and personal calls to action. Of why following your heart is not selfish, but your very reason for being and, that those who genuinely care about you, will love you for being true to what you need to fully embrace life. And ultimately, of why, when you commit to a chosen path the stars do align and your expectations are exceeded - again and again - and in ways you could never have imagined.

The individual stories that follow tell of *my version* of the people, places and events that stretched me; confronted me; taught me something; nourished me; made me cry in my bed or dance in the street over four incredible years. Others, who were there, may recall or interpret the very same things quite differently. Who can say where any one truth may lay and if, in the end, it matters anyway? Beyond this, all factual errors are mine.

I fulfilled a dream.

And it happened in Florence.

The Dream that Wouldn't Go Away

I was about to turn 50 and I was depressed. My friends and family, many of whom were much younger than me, thought this understandable. Why wouldn't a woman about to hit such a milestone be suitably down at years passed, youth lost forever, the prospect of naught but aging bones and more crows' feet? Their understanding and pity only made me feel worse. Because, vain as I am, this upcoming event was not the reason for my distress; advancing years had never been an issue for me and previous birthdays have only been a great excuse for chocolate cake and exotic travel. And yet, there was a connection with my unhappiness and my approaching birthday. It was simply this: *I was going to be 50 and I still hadn't taken my junior year abroad.*

I had always wanted to live outside the US, to speak a different language and *know* the European capitals. I wanted to be cultured, sophisticated, have that *je ne sais quoi*…I wanted to be Jackie Kennedy! Somehow I had missed the classic opportunities of being an exchange student in high school, and in college gotten waylaid by different kinds of 'cultural exchange' (like being a hippie and passing through phases of Hinduism, Buddhism and a few other trends of the day).

Making dreams and goals into reality is what I am known for and I see myself as someone who does this well. Being the youngest of three, with parents who had few aims for me other than to be pretty and make a great marriage, I'd always had to pursue and make happen for myself any extra-curricular activity that ranged beyond shopping. Dancing lessons or attending camp involved me doing the signing up, then begging for the funds from my father and nagging my mother to drive me to where I needed to be. The same applied to college applications. Although they of course wanted me to go to college, they simply didn't understand why I was choosing places as far away as I could get from the Detroit suburb where I lived,

There are plenty of good schools in Michigan Nita. Why can't you be content to do what all our friends' daughters are doing? (…becoming teachers to support their husbands through law or medical school.)

They just couldn't get why I wasn't happy to remain where I was.

My parents got an earlier taste of my intention to follow a different path when my 16th birthday had approached. My friends all had *Sweet Sixteen* parties at the country club or equally impressive venues. My mother, who loved to entertain, would have been thrilled to arrange such an event for me. But, I couldn't have cared less and insisted, instead, on celebrating this *passage* by spending the summer in Israel, traveling with a group, *Israel Tour for Teens*, and living on a kibbutz.

Once I felt the rush of international travel pulsing through my veins, there was no looking back. My high school peers saved money to buy make-up and clothes; I saved for my next *fix* - my next adventure, my next airline ticket.

The following year I was off with a group of 12 professionals; doctors, nurses, teachers and the young and not-yet professional me, to work on a community development project in a small village in Greece.

I was something of a hippie, long, straight hair parted in the middle, unshaven legs, hitchhiking whenever and wherever I could. All-in-all, I was not quite the Jewish princess my parents had hoped to be pairing up with a wealthy and, need I say, *Jewish* doctor.

Still, I was smart and a quick study, clear on my values and confident that anything was possible. I graduated top of my high school class and combined more travels with a succession of college, city, major (and boyfriend!) switches. I went to Tufts University in Boston; the University of Michigan; Marlboro College in Vermont and; following my BA, graduated from Mills College in the San Francisco area with (after majors in Art History, Sociology, Literature and Japanese Ceramics) a Masters in Dance Therapy. My changes in direction simply reflected my current passion, and the latest *revolution* or *in-thing*, clichéd maybe, but fascinating, fun and energizing.

When I was 24 and still studying, my mother died. She was 54. Her death was a devastating loss for me. It also changed my life forever: it was the catalyst that had me live life fully, never taking health, time, friendship, or love for granted. My priority became to do the things *worthy* of my life: things that fulfilled me, nourished me, satisfied my need for adventure, and made me appreciate the true joy and blessing of being alive. While my mother's death gave me the greatest lesson of my life, I would have happily traded the precious gift it brought me to have had her *in* my life for much, much longer. Still, the trade wasn't mine to make. The hard lesson her death provided was on the transience of life, that it could be cut short at any moment. The gift it had offered was the wake up call that led to my commitment that I would live a life without regrets for paths not followed and possibilities not grasped. Above all, my dreams would become realities.

The first big test of how I was living up to this commitment happened on my 30th birthday. I was crossing the San Francisco Bay Bridge on my way into work and I crashed into the car in front of me. My car was totaled. The event triggered a shocking insight: *that I was not living the life I wanted to be living.* In many respects I was happy. I had great friendships, fulfilling work, plenty of travel and adventure. But, I realized I no longer wished to experience these things alone. I wanted a passionate, adoring and fun relationship with a man with whom I could share all this richness.

When I thought about what a 30 year-old woman looked like, I imagined her married, kids and a station wagon (my mother was going on her third child at this age). It wasn't so much that I felt compelled to comply with this norm nor had any *need* to get married. But surely, a date would be nice, something I'd not actually had for going on five years!

When you're not looking, that's when you'll find him; I took my friends' advice…for two years. So that became two more years without a date, seven years in total, maybe some kind of a record?

I did some serious thinking. It became clear that my other accomplishments in life had not occurred when I *wasn't looking.* Tickets to Paris didn't drop into my mailbox when I least expected them, or a business engagement land in my lap when it was *just the right time.* In these and other cases, I'd actually *done something* to make them happen. It was time for action.

What I did next, how I did what I did, and the results of what I did (namely finding Tony my incredible, adorable, handsome husband) are the subject of my four books on relationships (see back of book). The lessons for me about being truly effective in reaching goals, discovered through my real life case study, were profound and provided the insights

I have applied to everything I've since set out to achieve in my life but…

…just when I thought there was no goal I couldn't reach, I was hit a curve ball. Tony and I wanted a family: *I couldn't get pregnant.* Like many women in this position I felt lacking and a failure as a woman. For two years I visited the fertility clinic. One day, humiliated at being turned away from my ultrasound because I hadn't quite managed to drink the requisite three-quarters of a gallon of water, I walked past, with great sadness, the other pitiful and, to me at that time, pathetic looking barren women in the waiting room. It hit me that I was looking into a mirror; they were a reflection of me.

Pathetic isn't my style. I don't *do victim* well. I made a decision then and there that I would take another path to reach the dream I shared with Tony. I asked myself a question I often pose with my consulting clients when challenging them to get into action with their goals: *are you committed to the process or the result?* Was I committed to getting pregnant or being a mom?

Tony was in agreement that the goal here was becoming parents and ten weeks later we shared the overwhelming experience of witnessing the birth of our adopted son, Jordan. Some years later I held Montana, my equally precious, also adopted, baby daughter in my arms. Tony and I had reached our goal, just not in the way we'd anticipated.

It was reflecting on the success, despite the many obstacles, of finding Tony and creating our family, as well as the achievement of my other goals in life, that left me, at 50, puzzled and depressed at not having achieved my dream of living in Europe.

My work at that time involved delivering a program which focused participants, mainly senior leaders, on the *quality* of how they spent time. It included the exercise: *If you had five years to live; one year to live; one month to live; one week to live...what would you do?* I asked the class to think about the dreams that, no matter how hard they tried to put aside, no matter how *impractical* they convinced themselves they were, no matter how *selfish* they felt for having them… just kept popping up again and again.

Of course, my longing to live in Europe was a shining example of one of these *will-not-go-away* dreams. I cautioned my clients against ignoring these at their peril; the acute pain and despondency of *regret* being the inevitable result if they did. As I approached my 50th birthday I was slapped with the realization, that of all the goals I had set in the past, this was the only one I had not achieved. It was me that was in peril! I felt I'd failed in some way, I hadn't *walked the talk* and I hadn't stayed true to myself and my commitment.

I could have made excuses and come up with reasons why I hadn't made this goal into a reality: family, career, money. But what purpose did excuses serve? And anyway, there was no one else asking me to justify my inaction; this was just about my relationship with me. *Living in Europe*: the dream wasn't going to go away, it was still a goal, and it needed to happen.

I pulled myself together for my birthday celebrations and had a fun time in New Orleans with Tony and friends. I counted my blessings and they were many. To give this half-century mark more meaning for myself, I sent a letter to my friends: *I know you all want to buy and lavish me with very expensive gifts…but*, then asked them to donate to a reading program for a child in an inner-city school, who already in second grade, could not read at all. They gave generously, and in addition, the Linda Mood-Bell organization reduced its fee for this highly effective six-week program that changes a child's neuro-pathways to achieve amazing results very quickly. A few months later I was lucky enough to meet the young girl who we'd sent through the program. Previously shy and unable to read even at a pre-school level, she was now entering the third grade reading *above* grade level! I shared her obvious excitement as she read me some passages from the Harry Potter book I'd brought her, the story now confidently at her command.

How I'd have loved to have made such rapid and significant progress with my dream of living in Europe. I wondered which neuro-pathways *I* needed to re-adjust to actually make it happen. Where, I wondered was the six-week program for me?

It took somewhat longer for me to achieve my goal, but it did happen.

It happened quite spectacularly in the end, though not for another four years...

With or Without Him

Tony was willing to move to Europe but there was a *right* way to do it, a *responsible* way. We needed a job or jobs, to support us while there, and a company that would pay for our moving expenses and for the kids schooling. *That* was the way it was done.

I took on the project of making this happen - the information gathering and job hunting. I subscribed to *The Financial Times* to look for overseas work opportunities and contacted people I knew who worked abroad for leads, contacts, introductions. And of course, I had *Plan B* at the back of my mind: *our ship will come in*. I religiously bought lottery tickets and day-dreamed about a surprise windfall from a long-forgotten investment or an inheritance from some rich and distant relative.

Two years passed with no suitable work lined up and no ships on the horizon.

Enough already! During my months of trying to find an overseas situation and waiting for *something* to happen, our closest friends from Santa Fe, did what we should have done and packed up their home and two kids and moved to Florence. We went to visit them several times. I got the *pleasure* of witnessing them living my dream *and* in the city which I was certain would be the ideal place for us!

Basta!

I was now 53, never forgetting that my mother had died at 54, the urgency to achieve my goal was suddenly tremendous. So, I dropped the bomb on Tony and Montana (Jordan now being off at college) announcing,

This must happen and it must happen now!

But it's not my dream to move to Italy, Tony responded. *Sure it would be nice, but we have a house here, you have a great job which you're risking if you leave, we should wait for a better time.*

Montana, not wanting to leave her friends for a scary unknown, had a more convincing argument for waiting,

I start high school in a year Mom; so if we are going to do this, it won't be so hard for me to do it then - I'll have to change schools anyway.

Montana's point, though clearly just a delay tactic for something she didn't want to happen at all, did make sense. I agreed to put things off, but not indefinitely, and declared to Tony,

One more year then we're going, no matter what! Montana and I are moving to Italy, we would love to have you with us, but we'll be going whether you come or not.

So, Tony got a respite, hoping that I would change my mind during the year, but when spring arrived, Montana and I went to Florence to look at the school she'd be attending and find housing for the next fall. On our return, Tony brought out the big guns,

We can't go; we don't have the money; we can't afford it; Montana doesn't want to go. And then, what he thought would be the lethal weapon,

What if I don't go, Nita?

He didn't receive the answer he expected,

We'll miss you.

He knew then that I was serious about going with or without him. He was tremendously hurt that I would actually do this and chose to interpret the situation as my not caring for him. I refused to shape the conversation in this way,

This is not about leaving you, or not loving you, or not being committed to you. I know I will make our marriage and family work no matter what. I am not leaving our marriage and I refuse to have this be a choice between our marriage and my dreams.

He held out, not making a commitment to go or stay.

Throughout the summer our friends had plenty to say… about Montana and I heading off to Florence later that year; about *possibly* going without Tony; about leaving at all. They were clearly upset,

How could you do this to Tony?

A few even took Montana aside and later confided to me,

Did you know that Montana doesn't actually want to go to Florence?

Honestly, I didn't have an issue with their judgments or their arguments as to why I couldn't possibly do such a thing. Of course, I knew that some people were personally confronted and made uncomfortable by my commitment. It made them face up to their having given up on making their own lifelong dreams into realities. Mostly though, I knew that our friends' comments came from a place of genuine concern, for me, for Tony and for the future of our family.

In terms of what was happening between Tony and me at this time, I knew that he wanted me to talk him into coming to Florence with us, to continue trying to convince him; to *sell* him on the idea. I had no interest in doing this. At the end of the day, if he made a choice to stay at home I would support that; if he wanted to come with us, then that would be magnificent, but I wanted *him* to be responsible for his *own* decision.

…besides, there was another reason I would not waste my words and energy on persuasion. I had some insider-information. Throughout all the discussions and conflict with friends and with Tony, both Montana and I knew, without a shadow of a doubt, a certainty of which even Tony remained quite unaware: *he would be coming to Florence with us.*

And then, incredibly, the proverbial ship came in. It arrived in the form of a handsome sum resulting from the re-mortgage of an investment property. We'd had no idea it would deliver such a significant windfall. Tony's greatest concern, how to fund the adventure, now removed, he was all set to go.

Of course, to this day, Montana and I knew he'd have come anyway…

Non Si Fa!

One of the things I love most about being somewhere new is *observing* and, in some but not all cases *absorbing*, the different attitudes, habits and taboos that attach themselves even to the most simple every day activities, especially relating to food and dress. An early lesson in Italy, involved becoming oriented to the rules of etiquette regarding going to the gym, something I regularly did in the US, getting up by 6:00am to arrive there well within the hour.

When first in Florence, I couldn't even find a gym that opened before 9.00am and so was able to justify a new routine, waking, guiltless, sometime around 8.30am. Then, just as I would back home, I'd put on my workout clothes and head off. In contrast to back home, arriving at the gym in Florence, I was the only one to get there ready for action. The Italians make their entrance in their work clothes, perfectly done hair and full make-up. Once there, they change into the appropriate workout attire, do their exercise, get dressed again and then go off to work. Some, but not all, take a shower, but there's rarely a need as they barely break a sweat!

Not only would I wear my workout clothes *to* the gym, I'd wear them for my bike ride back afterwards and, still in my sweats, stop off for my morning cappuccino. Everything about this, I learned, was *non si fa* - never to be done. Though I continued to wear my workout clothes to and from the gym, not being able to tolerate two extra changes, I soon became too uncomfortable to sit in a café *undressed*. It was just as awkward as if I was sitting there wearing my pajamas.

Tony had a similar lesson on dress etiquette when he joined a group to play tennis. He was told that they started at 7.00pm. He arrived at the club at 6:45pm in his tennis attire and went out to the court. No one else was there. He walked back into the club to see several men in business suits, drinking coffee and chatting. He was the only one in shorts. It wasn't until sometime after 8.00pm that *play* actually commenced. He felt out of place and very embarrassed.

I soon discovered other dress related *non si fa* taboos including wearing country clothes in the city and vice versa. It's not just a case of *smart* versus *casual*; it's much more complex. For example, jeans are OK for *city casual* (shorts are *never* OK in the city even in roasting August) but *country casual* means khakis. Once, when invited to a hunt, my Italian host, in an aside to his son who would be escorting me, and not knowing that I spoke Italian, prompted,

Make sure she has the right clothes.

Obviously he wanted to avoid any embarrassment on both sides if I turned up dressed *inappropriately*. Since I'd been on a hunt before, and by that time was fairly schooled in the commandment of *la bella figura* - the need to *look good*, I laughed as I provided assurance that I knew exactly what was required of me. I was quite aware not to make the mistake of thinking *hunting attire* would be the same as *country casual*. I also knew that I would need to drive to the event in *one* pair boots, before changing into a *second* kind to actually hunt, and then make sure I had a *third* pair lined up ready to slip into before partaking of the post-hunt refreshments.

Going back to the *casual* thing, there are even further sub-sets to consider. As well as *city casual*, there's *beach casual* and different etiquette again surrounding appropriate attire for a trip to the mountains. And no event can ever be considered casual enough to warrant bare feet, even in the house; *especially* in front of guests, shoes or slippers of some kind are a must at all times.

When it came to food, there were many things I learned about *what should never be done,* typified by the law-like dictate of not having parmesan cheese on seafood pasta. One evening in Rome, I chose not to do as the Romans do. The seafood dish I'd ordered was uncomfortably spicy and I hoped that maybe some parmesan would have a cooling effect on the heat of the chili. I knew it was *wrong* but was happy to throw caution to the wind in order to enjoy my meal. Explaining my plight, I politely asked the waiter if he could please bring me some parmesan. I may as well have asked if I could have some clippers to cut my toenails at the table. *No,* apparently I could *not* have some parmesan.

He simply wouldn't bring it.

I still wanted it.

When he was out of sight, I looked around for the *forbidden fruit.* I could see it, almost within reach, a small bowl on the table where the cutlery and other condiments were kept. Like a thief in the night, I crept up and snatched it away. I almost expected an alarm bell to go off and an angry mob of security guards to descend upon me. However, I successfully made it back to the table and sprinkled the illicit substance on my dinner. The second the waiter noticed my infraction, the container was whisked away, presumably so that he could eliminate the risk that witnesses would testify he was in any way involved in the offending scenario. If I'd have asked for my leftovers in a doggie bag, another *non si fa,* this would have been beyond pushing my luck.

There are many other food *not-tos* for a visitor to Italy to navigate, such as mixing different foods on the same plate as opposed to serving them on separate dishes and hence the terms *primo piatto* and *secondi piatti* and the separate vegetable dishes that you'll find on menus. Something else you'll observe, when eating out or at someone's home, is that if flavors and textures are to be combined this should only be done in tried, tested, and therefore traditional ways. For instance, sweet should never meet sour in an Italian dish, though Italians will happily enjoy the combination when eating Chinese food. And don't make the mistake of thinking that you can have *whatever you like* in a deli where you're invited to choose your own sandwich fillings! Even if it's what your heart most desires, it's hard to argue with the logic, for example, that while you will happily be served tomato with mozzarella, there are many other fillings you will not be allowed to partner with tomato, on the basis *it will make the sandwich soggy*.

Whatever you do, don't even think about taking your lunchtime sandwich on the run. There's a proper time and place to eat and that isn't at your desk; on the street; driving in a car; riding on a bus; or traveling on a train other than when in the dining car. Eating requires going to a *proper* place to do it, usually at home or a restaurant, but always at a table, and *paying attention* to the food as you eat (no gossiping into your mobile in between mouthfuls). The same focus is given to the smoking of a cigarette or the eating of an ice-cream. Food consumption and shopping are also not to be mixed; you won't find food courts at shopping malls unlike in the US where they often seem to be the main event.

A spin-off from the need to eat at a table, I also discovered that, apart from the mid-afternoon *merenda* of young children, *snacking* appeared to be an all too casual way to treat food and, again, *just isn't done*. I only really struggled with the lack of a snacking mentality when it came to going to see Italian films in the local movie houses as often there were no eat-treats available at all - not even popcorn! The Odeon, however, which shows movies in English several nights a week, can not only be relied upon for the usual popcorn and candy, you are also able to enjoy the movie with a small bottle of wine and a selection of gourmet chocolates - very civilized.

And, of all things *non si fa* to remember on a trip to Italy, be prepared for a look of abject horror on the face of a waiter or barista if you request a cappuccino *after* your meal. This will amount to an incomprehensible act of madness to an Italian. Milky coffee is viewed as a *breakfast* drink only so, in their eyes, you may as well be asking to have a bowl of cereal, insulting the host or chef by more or less announcing to everyone that you were not fed enough at the meal. And if you *truly* want to signal your total lack of familiarity with *what simply isn't done* on the dining front, combine your request for an after-dinner cappuccino with the further instruction that you'd like it in a *to-go* cup! I dare you.

Be Careful What You Wish For

During our first few weeks in Florence, Tony and I avidly followed the news of the 2004 US election campaign in the *International Herald Tribune*. We were fortunate to have access to this English language paper at such a critical time for our country. We also devoured the other international news it covered. Yet, from very early in our stay, we were hungry for local news too. We wanted to know what was happening in Italy, and naturally enough, in Florence, the city we'd chosen to make our home. How else could we connect with the local community, feel a part of it?

We knew, of course, that learning the language was critical to achieving a greater sense of belonging and involvement. We attended Italian lessons and were brave and improving daily in our interactions while buying food in the market, trying to get our internet connected, or figuring out the mysteries of the bus and train systems. Yet, we were obviously a long way off from being able to scan the front pages of *La Nazione* or *La Republica* and join in animated café conversation about the latest political scandal or cultural discovery. Where would we get hold of the news we craved until such a day arrived?

Tony was clear on the matter,

Florence should have a newspaper like the one we used to get in San Miguel de Allende.

That summer in Mexico we'd pour over its pages every Thursday to find out about up-coming events, but more importantly to get up to speed with the local news. This had helped us feel a part of life there and not just tourists observing from the outside how others lived. We'd come across similar papers elsewhere on our travels throughout the world. Paris, Amsterdam and Barcelona, even Bucharest had a daily English language newspaper. I refused to believe that something similar didn't already exist in Florence. Surely, such a major city, to which the English speaking nations of the world have been flocking for centuries, would have something to keep its news starved non-Italian speaking population informed?

No, there was nothing.

So we had identified a gap in the market and my gorgeous, savvy, businessman of a husband decreed that *someone* should fill it. I agreed, pointing out to *him* what was obvious to *me*,

You do realize that the 'someone' you're referring to is you?

As far as I was concerned it was the perfect project for Tony. Not only could he see the value and potential of such a newspaper, but it was an opportunity for him to get his sleeves rolled up and be productive. Tony is a bit hyperactive and if he isn't busy, he's not happy, nor fun to be with.

The transition to our new life in Italy had been much easier for me than Tony. I carried on my management consulting work with the same group of multinationals and just flew off now and then to wherever in the world my next contract took me. In contrast, Tony had arrived in Florence without work, not quite sure how he would make a living, but imagining to begin with, given our recent windfall, that like many before him arriving in Italy, he might do *a bit of painting*.

The reality was, that while others would give a right arm for a relaxing sabbatical in foreign climes, Tony shines when he has a strong purpose and focus and something significant to accomplish. It soon became apparent he was beginning to drift and struggling to adjust to a life without obvious or specific aims. Tony needed a job. I needed a more fulfilled husband. Montana needed a happier dad. The ex-pats and tourists of Florence needed local news.

It had begun.

Labor Pains

If the newspaper had been *my* project I'd have been on the phone finding advertisers, contacting a printer and writing the first editorial on the morning of day one. Tony's approach to getting things done is somewhat different than mine and so his first steps seemed unnecessary and annoyed me: *doing due diligence.* He set out to gather the evidence, assess the facts, evaluate the options and make sure that, beyond being a good idea, the paper actually could be a viable venture.

Tony sought information and advice from those experienced in the world of newspapers and magazines. One friend in the US, who owns a successful magazine himself, instructed that market research and analysis of the local demographics was critical. Another friend simply advised,

Don't do it, it'll never make any money.

People around us in Florence smiled indulgently, two more America dilettantes with a crazy idea that'd never come to anything - just a new twist on a *bit of painting.*

I believed that no amount of data and number crunching would prove or disprove that something that hadn't been done before (in Florence) would work or not; you just had to do it and see what happened. For me, the pull of something new and exciting *and* worthwhile was just too great.

Looking back, one way in which I had rationalized, to myself, my failure to get to Europe sooner was the lack of a specific *raison d'être*, a job, something to study, a specific project; a way to be involved. After 54 years, none of these had arisen, so I'd finally reframed my purpose into: *the experience of living in another country and giving Montana exposure to the European culture.* However, if the newspaper came to fruition, it would fulfill me in a way that went to the heart of my personal mission to be doing something useful and making a difference. When it came to pursuing the idea of the newspaper, the biggest risk of all as far as I could see, was the lost opportunity of *not* going for it.

As Tony continued his research, looking into how to get venture capital, negotiating the legalities and the thousand other *how-to* challenges, I continued to travel doing my consulting work. Returning to Florence after giving a workshop in Hungary, I was thinking about the newspaper. At this point, Tony was losing steam, overwhelmed about *what* and *how* he needed to research before even deciding whether to actually pursue the venture at all.

In my recent workshop I'd been teaching: *how to make things happen,* basically what I call the technology of accomplishment. I realized that the way Tony was going about things was contrary to all that I'd just been coaching i.e. to make a commitment *first* and *then* figure out how to do it. Maybe Tony just couldn't do things this way, but I could. I got off the plane and told him *I* was committed to making the newspaper happen. My declaration had the effect of re-energizing Tony and the project took on a new momentum.

In between my work abroad, I continued with my Italian lessons. Catia is so much more than a great Italian teacher. During our lessons, she would have me talk about my day, what was most on my mind, my thoughts and beliefs on a wide range of subjects; we chatted away in my new language. Though I'm not a natural linguist, I have such a strong desire to communicate that I'm somehow able to make myself understood, even when not always accurate or elegant. These conversations would lead to me sharing various intimacies such as telling a story about my kids or a disagreement with a friend, or even an event from my own childhood; they'd also lead to tears! I was surprised to learn that, contrary to stereotype, Italians aren't as emotional as I'd expected. The fact that many Americans, and most definitely me, wear their hearts on their sleeves, actually makes many Italians question the sincerity of the emotions they witness us displaying. I'm sure Catia knew I was *for real*, but she'd try to steer the subject away from the likes of Montana, or Tony, or money, or the beauty of art…but no subject was entirely safe with me,

Nita! You're not going to cry again?

Any tears would usually be followed by us both collapsing into laughter.

During one of my lessons Catia shared a personal experience of how Italians are often puzzled by American expressiveness. Before she became a language teacher, she and her husband, Leo, owned a T-shirt store. American tourists would come in off the street, look at the T-shirts and exclaim,

Oh these are fantastic! They're so great! These are the best T-Shirts I've ever seen, really original, wonderful!

And then…they'd walk out without buying, leaving Leo and Catia dumbstruck.

I'd cycle to my lessons at Catia's studio near Piazza Santo Spirito, in the Oltrarno, the old artisan district. Now considered a hip area, places such as Catia husband's graphic design business, reflect its creative traditions. She held her lessons in a room above its premises.

A bathroom break from the torture of conjugation provided me with comic relief. I would need to go downstairs and walk through the office where Leo, Catia's husband, worked with his business partners, Marco and Giovanni. The trio was quick-witted with a wicked sense of humor and a great line in repartee. Leo was the artist, slightly rumpled, not always shaven, six foot three inches, huggable and very sexy (his brilliant caricature paintings of famous people adorned the walls). Marco was the make-it-happen business and marketing brains, handsome in a more typically Italian way. And Giovanni was the 'operations director', tall, sandy-haired, a bit more English looking in appearance which suited his dry, acerbic wit.

The price to pay for a chance to banter with this smart and gorgeous threesome was their merciless teasing about, well about anything and everything….my clothing, what I ate, how much I paid for something and plenty connected to my being American. About my Italian, Leo, in particular, had much to say, pleading with me not to let anybody know that his wife was my teacher or she'd be put out of business, *Please, for my children's sake!*

I tried to give just as good as I got, but it would have been a hard enough achievement in my first language let alone my halting Italian. I also knew that even in English, these guys were quicker, sharper and funnier than I could ever hope to be.

It was on one of these entertaining bathroom visits, after I had made my declaration that the newspaper was going to happen and I'd leapt fully into the *doing-it* phase, I'd asked Leo where I could get printing done. I was looking for something like a Kinko's in the US. When he asked what work I needed doing, we fell into a conversation about Tony's English newspaper idea.

Soon after, Leo sent me an e-mail saying they were interested in the project and wanted to get involved. Tony and I went to meet them. Marco and Leo were very enthusiastic. The third partner in crime, Giovanni, was not. He warned us of various bureaucratic hoops we hadn't a hope of jumping through and I became familiar with a phrase I would hear from him a thousand times over the next few years: *è difficile*. Printing costs would be high, he advised. It would be particularly challenging to obtain the necessary *Director Responsible* permit, a piece of paper authorizing someone as the official head of a publication. To be granted this permit, a person needed a number of years experience as a journalist, specific qualifications, and proof of having conducted a minimum quantity of interviews.

Despite their partner's reticence, it was Leo and Marco's enthusiasm that won the day and Tony too was ready to go ahead. A short while later the ever-serious Giovanni explained to me that they had found a printer for about a third of the cost of what we'd anticipated and that the same people were also able to provide a *Director Responsible* permit. I was confused at his solemn expression and tried to find out if I was missing something,

So you're telling me that you got the printing cost to lower than we even budgeted? That's a good thing, isn't it?

Yes, he confirmed.

So why do you look like your cat just got run over? You need to inform your face that it should be looking happy.

I soon got used to Giovanni starting every meeting with those seemingly discouraging words: *è difficile*. However, I learned not to translate his comment literally, as in *it's difficult,* but to extend the definition to: *it was very difficult, but I've found a solution.* And each time I heard those words, I would sit back and patiently wait to hear how he overcame heroic odds to save the day, a talent for which I would come to love and adore Giovanni.

Without an agreement of how we would work together, own the newspaper and divide the labor, responsibilities and costs, we all got to work on bringing it into existence. None of us had had newspaper experience. When it came down to it, Tony and I had no idea who our partners really were. Friends warned us to be careful,

Shouldn't you get a legal document drawn up or at least something in writing? How can you be sure you're not falling prey to the stereotypical scenario of dishonest, corrupt Italians taking advantage of rich, gullible Americans?

For Tony and me, there was no question we were working with the *right* people. We were having so much fun with these guys and feeling a part of making something special happen *and* truly living an Italian life, that we threw caution, happily and knowingly, to the wind.

Slow Food

Every morning in Florence, I'd to go out for un caffè. Of course I have the luxury of a cappuccino anytime, anywhere in LA, but it just doesn't taste the same if it's not made by the masterful Isadoro at *Cibreo*. He makes it to my exact requirements, perfectly every time. Isadoro knows me, my family and my friends and, when I was looking for a new apartment, he had a new lead and phone number for me every day until I found one. Unless I was meeting a friend, like most Italians, I soon got used to standing up at the bar, drinking my cappuccino quickly and when my Italian was up to it, sharing a few words on the political situation or latest scandal with Isadoro and the other bar patrons, before heading off to work.

Cibreo is adjacent to another favorite place, Mercato Sant' Ambrogio. I soon became a regular, buying fruit and vegetables from the outdoor stalls and venturing inside to find fish, cheese, meat and poultry. I preferred shopping there to the Mercato Centrale because it was nearer to my home and I liked its smaller size. It wasn't long before I found myself frequenting the same stalls, developing relationships and being taken care of by the vendors.

I am famous, or rather infamous, in both the US and Italy for not cooking. At the same time, I've managed to pull off a reputation as a great hostess who always has splendid food on her table. This has largely been achieved by getting expert at buying scrumptious already prepared food. In Italy, there is something of a skill attached to this (really!) as there's very little available as compared to the US.

In winter, I lived on *ribollita*, a thick, hearty bean and vegetable soup. You're certain to find a great recipe for it in Frances Mayes' *Under the Tuscan Sun*. My friendly vendor from whom I purchased what in the US we'd call minestrone, always reminded me that I could reheat it as many times as I wanted; *ribollita* means re-boiled.

Buying food at the market always led to a barrage of questions,

How many people are you serving? When are you eating this? What are you serving to accompany it? What wine are you drinking with it? How are you cooking it?

Purchasing a piece of meat from the butcher is kindred to adopting a pet from the Humane Society; until he is assured that you will be taking proper care of the purchase, he isn't going to let you have it. And with fruit, buying a melon for example, the first question would be,

When are you eating it - today, tomorrow?

And depending on my answer, the vendor would make a selection and hand me over a fruit of the appropriate ripeness. If my answer gave a date three days out or more, she'd look at me like I was joking,

Why would you come to the market today? Come back when you actually need it.

In addition to getting the meat, fruit and vegetables that *exactly* met my needs, my responses to other interrogations would ensure that I got the *right* kind of pesto to have with the bruschetta I was serving, and *not* the one more suited to eat with pasta; the *correct* amount of sauce to accompany the fresh linguine I'd chosen; and the *best* advice on the way to prepare, cook and serve all the things I'd purchased on any given day.

One afternoon, early in my time in Florence, I visited a deli, the market being closed (a challenge because in the US I was more used to after-work grocery shopping). This store sold cheese, ham, salami, pasta, sauces and the like. When it was my turn to be served, I was asked what I would come to discover as the *usual* questions. During the course of the conversation with the vendor I was invited to taste different sauces and meats, a process somewhat lengthened by my then very beginner's Italian. I looked behind to see that other patrons had entered the shop. They were soon weighing in on the conversation, giving their opinions on anything and everything related to my purchases, arguing with each other as well as with the shopkeeper. I was surrounded by experts…few of them agreed with each other.

I began to feel a little embarrassed taking so much time, tasting, comparing and choosing. My sense of unease was compounded by the fact that in Italy, a stallholder or shopkeeper (or clerk for that matter), doesn't placate waiting customers with: *I'll be with you in a minute* or *if you just want bread, I can take care of that quickly for you.* Instead, they wait on one person at a time, not even paying the slightest attention to anyone else until that person is completely served.

What struck me most about my visit to the market that day was that the other customers showed no signs of irritation or impatience. When I apologized they asked: *What for?* I thought of how I'd have reacted, back in the US, in a similar situation. In fact, I knew how I would feel, because it's a common experience. When I'm at the check-out counter and the cashier is friendly or, even worse, turns out to *know* the person in front of me and gets into a conversation, I get in a huff, look at my watch and sigh loudly. Not infrequently, I have dropped my items right at the counter and walked out of the store in frustration or simply because I fear missing my next appointment.

I have to admit when shopping in Italy today, I still find the lack of acknowledgement by a salesperson a challenge. The only difference now is that I'm one of the authoritative throng who unabashedly weighs in with my opinion.

The Face that Launched a Thousand Issues

We soon settled on the name for our venture: *The Florentine*. Leo had been asking us what content we wanted to have in the newly named paper and what we'd like from a design point of view. Tony went into his research mode. Meanwhile, I took a copy of the Mexico newspaper I was using as our model and cut and pasted different columns together with titles like *classified, news, sports* and *events* and so created a rough mock-up. Tony couldn't stand the results of my inexact and sloppy work so he painstakingly spent three days on his computer, measuring columns, word count and the ratio of advertisements to editorial and column inches.

I was about to drop off both of our masterpieces when an e-mail from Leo popped into my inbox: *just something I put together in ten minutes.* Tony and I saw, in format and color, a layout that is remarkably close to the exquisite design of *The Florentine* still being used today with its distinctive masthead, Florentine lily motifs and tasteful palette. It was the moment I saw this version - in full color - that I knew, without a doubt, the paper was going to happen.

These original ideas were developed further into a few mock-ups, and while I could clearly see the paper was shaping up to be a thing of beauty, I had concerns. To me, it had more the appearance of a fashion magazine than a newspaper and there was just *too much going on*. This highlighted the fact that the guys' primary focus was on the *appearance* of the paper, rather than its actual *content*; after all, they already knew the news from Italian newspapers. Their biggest concern was that, at all costs, *The Florentine* didn't look *boring*. These first layouts had columns, boxes, headlines, and color all over the place. In addition, articles were cut up in two sections, sometimes more, starting on one page to be continued on another. The overall confusion created a look that, surely, I argued, would only appeal to readers with attention-deficit disorder. I grabbed a copy of the rather more prosaic looking *New York Times* and waved it in front of them,

I get plenty of 'beautiful' in Italy, what I'm missing, what I'm craving is this - I want words that I can read, understand, that will inform me.

We reached a compromise. Although my partners knew for sure that I was going to bore the readers to death, with the exception of the front page, they indulged me by keeping the articles whole and in one place and made the overall look considerably less frenetic.

The Florentine was, and still is, visibly beautiful. I take no credit for this. If it had been up to me, it would have been a black and white simple gazette, and this would have proved a fatal error (explaining why I was subsequently excluded from all matters of aesthetics). Our target readership, the English-speaking ex-pats and tourists, I knew would be satisfied with a no-frills appearance. For them, like me, it was the content that would be critical. But, in order to ensure that what was to be a free paper, was prominently displayed and widely distributed by the *Italian* businesses that we hoped would prove willing to do so, the overall *look* of *The Florentine* would be critical.

I'd had previous instruction on the importance of *looking good* in my new country of residence. *Fare la bella figura* was more a cultural commandment than a piece of advice - *thou shalt look good!* Having been trained in psychology and after decades of working with people and their egos in business, the concept of the need to look good was certainly not new to me. It is however, in my experience, usually considered a sinister trait, something which people tend to deny, hide or try to overcome. In the business world if, as a leader, you focus on yourself and what others think of you, this is generally viewed as a sure way to sabotage success. Of course, to some extent, all human beings want to look good in the eyes of others and certainly people rarely set out with the intention of looking bad. But, in Italy, I was repeatedly surprised by the extent to which outward appearances played a significant role in how people were judged.

If you believe that how you look physically, the way you dress, with whom you mix and at which places you socialize and eat, are all of no importance whatsoever; and if you are offended by personal judgments made on the basis of such things and are not able to find some way of coming to terms with others frequently doing this, then I recommend you choose another country to love and adore. In Italy, the key to your reputation and your success - both personally and financially - is an understanding of, and obedience to, the laws of looking good. And they have no shame about this. None!

It was on an earlier trip to Italy, before we'd taken up residence, that I'd been offered some insights into the origination of the importance of *la bella figura* in Italy. We had hired a private guide for our family's visit to the Vatican and Coliseum. The young, and of course gorgeous, *Prada*-suited Italian, was an art history professor at one of the US universities in Rome. In his informative discourse about a pre-Christian painting, he explained that the Vatican's historians rationalized the symbolism in the scene before us as a prophecy of the coming of Christianity. His tone sounded distinctly cynical and so I probed him for what he *wasn't* saying. He opened up,

Of course, I'm Catholic, like all Italians, but I have no admiration, nor respect for the Church, what they have done throughout history, and what they continue to do today. The Church is not about religion and spirituality or humanitarianism. It has been, is, and always will be, about money and power.

Where the painting itself had completely failed to get our kids' attention, they were now rapt by the guide's fierce and cutting words,

The one good thing about the Church, for which I am eternally grateful, as it has given me my livelihood, is its appreciation of art and visual beauty. Other cultures destroyed pagan art and antiquities; the Catholic Church co-opted it, and justified preserving this profound beauty by inventing some garbage (he waves his hand at the painting) *proclaiming that a certain hand gesture, or the focus of the eyes, foretold the 'Coming of Christ'.*

There was no stopping him,

If you look at, or just think about Italy's offerings to the world, they're almost all visual; sculpture, painting, textiles. Still today, the country is known for the beautiful design of cars, furniture, fashion. Everything has to look good, and this all originated from the Church.

Yes, everything has to look good; this lesson was instructive when it came to *The Florentine*. Very early on, I realized it was *because* of the impressive and elegant appearance my partners insisted upon, that the luxurious Lungarno hotels wanted to have copies of the paper in every room for their guests. This was also why hip restaurants and stores were more than happy to display them on their counters and coffee tables. Not to mention that without the right *look* we wouldn't have had a hope in hell of selling any advertisements to Italian businesses. If *The Florentine* looked good, it could make them look good which, at the end of the day, is all that mattered.

No Lions, No Tigers, No Boars, Oh My!

Proverbial wisdom about *early birds catching worms* doesn't apply to boar hunting. At 9.00am the hunters were just starting to arrive. I was there at the invitation of the successful vintner Francesco Mazzei, who I'd met at a social gathering. When he heard I'd never attended a boar hunt he asked me along and, as usual, I was excited by the opportunity not only to be there, but to afterwards write an article about this authentic Tuscan experience for *The Florentine* readers.

The countryside in Maremma, southwest Tuscany, is spectacular, but even more compelling to my eyes was the parade of men gathered for the hunt, from seven year-old Luca, joining in for the first time, through to the 80 year-old veteran Stefano. Their hunting garb featured rich greens and browns; suede coats, luscious cashmere sweaters, scarves and hats were all layered with casual elegance. Armani, styling a hunt for a movie, would have been hard pushed to improve upon the overall effect and indeed, probably had some hand in it anyway! Each of the well-attired men to whom I was introduced, lifted my hand to his lips in greeting. I was one of 4 women amongst 70 men. Sometimes life is very good indeed.

A membership of this particular hunt costs approximately €1000 entitling the hunter to participate twice a year. To keep them in the area, the boars are fed year-round.

Through a lottery system, each hunter is assigned to a numbered stand and people leave for their post by foot or on the back of a type of hay wagon. The leader makes certain each hunter finds his spot and offers the traditional words for good luck,

In boca al lupo!

This literally translates to: *in the mouth of the wolf.* The hunter must answer with a resounding,

Crepi! May the wolf die!

Wolves! Who said anything about wolves?

Because my host, Francesco, had organized the hunt, he was able to pick a prime spot for us on top of a small hill, with a 360 degree view of the countryside, forest and sea. We climbed up the ladder to our tree house, a four by four platform with railings and a bench. After making sure I was seated and safe, Francesco took a machete and climbed down again. He cleared away some of the brush around our site so that we'd be able to more clearly see any of the boar that passed our way.

Once the horn signaled the start of the hunt, groups of men, called beaters, with 50 dogs in each group, tracked the boars and beat them out of the bush and into the view of the hunters. My host explained that you hunt the boars with your ears,

You hear the dogs barking louder and the leaves rustling. The dogs become more frantic as soon as they are on the tail of the boar. The difference between the sound of a dog running and the sound of a boar running is the noise, in the latter case, of branches cracking under the weight.

So we waited, listened and then heard a boar come very close. Francesco pointed his rifle where he thought it would appear; hunters have to be ready to shoot the second the boar comes into sight, there's no time to take aim *after* you first see it. We waited, and listened, he aimed; we waited, we listened, he aimed…for four hours. My sense of excitement and anticipation dissipated after about the first hour and so I settled in to enjoy the scenery, invigorating country air and the company of my host. Francesco liked hunting boars because, he shared,

It isn't a sure thing - it takes skill and patience, you have to be attentive and listen, it's almost meditative.

Suddenly, he broke off our conversation, put his finger to his lips and lifted his gun. The sound of the boar's movement was just as Francesco had described. I couldn't see the beast but I knew it was close. Just as he poised to shoot, the sound of cracking branches receded, the boar changed its direction and our would-be target disappeared before it had appeared at all. Francesco grabbed me by the shoulders and sniffed my neck,

Are you wearing perfume?

Fortunately, I understood his abrupt behavior because I'd been forewarned about not wearing scent or even showering with soap before the hunt; one whiff of an unfamiliar odor is apparently enough to send the boar racing in the opposite direction. The hunter may depend on his ears for success, but the boar, it seemed, depended on its nose for its very survival.

Though we never killed anything that day, we heard shooting all around us. As we walked back down the road, I asked Francesco if now was the time when everyone got to tell their hunting stories; how they shot and either missed or struck the boar. Francesco nodded, that was exactly what would take place next over the luncheon spread. I warned him,

I may not speak Italian fluently, but I understand everything, so if you blame the loud and perfumed American woman for spoiling your chances of shooting a boar, I will know!

We arrived back at the camp and I felt like a soldier returning from the war. We sat down to long tables overflowing with meat, including boar, just-baked bread, pecorino and mozzarella cheeses and several hot dishes. Everyone was tired but in great spirits. Food eaten and stories shared, the last part of the hunt experience consisted of watching while the 48 boars that had been shot that day, were hung, skinned and quartered. The beaters were paid in meat and then the hunters took whatever they wanted. Anything left is sold to local butchers.

I left satiated with the authentic local experience, the food, the friendship and a tale to tell *The Florentine* readers.

Destiny's Child

It was November when we all gave the green light to *The Florentine*. At one of our early meetings Giovanni asked me when I would like the first issue to come out. I didn't hesitate,

March!

Marco and Giovanni responded in unison and alarm,

Of what year?

We didn't get it out in March, but we did get it out on April 25th and knowing now what I do about getting things done in Italy, I realize my target date was insanely unrealistic; this would have been a challenging timescale even in America. Looking back I have no idea how we did it, but probably not knowing any better was an asset. In my impatient American way I just operated with a sense of urgency and expected things could be done. I can still see Giovanni, his hands in prayer, pleading with me,

Nita, Nita, Nita, you must understand, è difficile.

But fortunately my partners liked to pull rabbits out of hats, the April launch date was a triumph, a miracle was achieved.

Working on the first issue of *The Florentine*, the guys' focus was on the lay-out and overall appearance; mine on collecting the information and helping Tony choose the articles to create quality content; and Tony's, looking for advertisers and generally *getting the paper out*. We decided we would put out an issue once a week on Thursday (this would later change to every two weeks). The 24-page format included local news and sports coverage (we'd leave the world news to the *International Herald Tribune*); feature articles to cover topics such as art, history, food, wine, politics, travel and culture; comprehensive events pages; advertising, including classifieds; and another vital page (according to me, but not the guys) titled: *Important Numbers,* which listed contact numbers and website details for English speaking doctors, embassies, emergency services and churches.

While our Italian partners made progress with the design of *The Florentine*, given that it was going to be free, Tony looked to filling the paper with advertising, taking the first steps to making it a financially viable concern. Though he wasn't able to fill all the available ad space - a tall order for any first edition - he did have some significant wins with Volvo and a number of smaller local businesses taking the opportunity to promote their products and services.

I still had a number of consulting commitments which took me away from Florence and *The Florentine*, and while I had no specific role on the paper, I was immediately involved in helping put the content together. I wanted to make sure that the newspaper delivered on the aims we'd discussed when coming up with the idea: to deliver Italian news in English and to positively impact the quality of the experience ex-pats and tourists had during their time in Florence.

We hired a managing editor and she began to go through the Italian papers for the local news and suggest articles that Tony and I would approve and which she would then translate into English. In the first issue we included articles covering restoration plans for the Uffizi Gallery; details of new traffic restrictions in the city; controversy surrounding the April 25th Italian Liberation Day holiday; rent increases pushing out businesses from the city center; and soccer violence in Italian stadiums. We also included a number of *news in brief* items.

As well as news, we wanted several feature articles in the launch edition. Many of these pieces were written, all without payment, by friends, referrals, established writers and anyone who'd heard about the up-coming paper and wanted to contribute. We kicked off with articles about the mysteries of Italian street numbering; the wonderful Italian phrase *non te la prendre - don't take it seriously* (I was to hear that one many times from my colleagues); an intriguing Medici story; and an introduction to Tuscan cooking.

I knew that one of the biggest draws for our readers would be the events section; it was to turn out to be the hardest and most tedious work of the week. In my determination to provide a comprehensive service to our readers, I was involved in these pages from the beginning. There are a few events-type magazines in Florence as well as *a calendar magazine* in the Friday editions of all the Italian daily papers. However, even the Italians are confused by the incomplete, inconsistent and bordering on inaccurate presentation of times, dates, locations and details of how to purchase tickets. Some events are organized by venue, some by date, others, by the nature of the event. When it came to this section in *The Florentine* I was intent on accuracy, clarity and listing events day by day, to make planning easy for the readers.

My intention wasn't without its challenges. For example, when it came to the local markets (other than the everyday food markets) there is a monthly schedule for the regular antique, flower and flea markets. The timetabling itself (never mind the listing) was a mystery: the Arezzo antique market is held on the first weekend of every month; the market in Piazza dei Ciompi on the last Sunday; another crafts market on the second weekend; yet another on the third Thursday.

My Italian colleague Elia, who was in charge of the events section, wanted to follow the usual conventions of Italian magazines and websites and so list, in every issue, and within one box of text, the markets for the whole month. I said fine, *but*...I also insisted that if, for example, the monthly Arezzo market was happening during the week of that issue of the paper, it should *also* be listed under the separate *Sunday* heading. Elia thought I was being ridiculous. I tried, in vain, to explain that I just wanted to make it easy for the readers so they didn't have to spend time working out which week of the month it was or, worse, hop on a train to Arezzo to find they were a week early for the market. The latter would happen if they'd failed to use their psychic powers to realize that if the last day of the month fell on a Saturday, making Sunday the 1st, then this still counted as the *last* weekend of the month and so the market would not be held on this day.

Elia would persist in doing the listings *her way*, so I would correct the proofs to *my way* only to enjoy the fury of Leo unhappy at having to make so many last minute changes to the pages. Elia would also be angry, not just with me, but with all those *stupid and lazy Americans that need their hands held to get to a market*. It wasn't the first, or last, American-Italian culture clash that we'd experience on the paper. In this case I was delighted that my insistence on the way the event pages went out was validated. Not only did we get immediate and positive feedback from our target market, within a few months, we discovered that *Italians* were picking up our newspaper for the events section, *because it's the only user-friendly place you can find out what's going on.*

Still, such challenges aside, we somehow managed to fill the pages of the first issue. We were also able to include, with pride, a message of support from Eugenio Giani, (the wonderfully titled *City Councilor for International Relations, Valorization of Popular Traditions, Sports and Free Time Activities*) explaining how he saw the launch of *The Florentine* as an important means of communication to help orient and integrate Florence's many guests. In our own welcome we stated our goals for the readers:

To facilitate their ability to get news and information about the place where they were living or visiting; to organize clearly, in one place, and entirely in English, all events and activities; and to provide articles on Florence, Tuscany and Italy that were helpful, informative and entertaining.

So there it was, hot off the press, the first issue of *The Florentine*, a thing of beauty…and, we believed, quality.

But it was all for nothing unless we got it out there.

Tony loaded up his backpack and bicycle and set off on a delivery route to the various shops, businesses, hotels and public places where we hoped people would see *The Florentine* and pick it up. As he cycled away, his comment:

My first job was delivering newspapers, and here I am, almost 60 years old, and still a paperboy!

Montana and her friends got in on the act, taking copies of that first edition across the city. One of their distribution responsibilities was to hand them out to the captive audience in line at the theater that showed English language films three nights a week. Montana, herself then going in to watch the film, described her teenage embarrassment when, sitting inside, waiting for the movie to start, she looked around to see *everyone reading my Mom's newspaper.*

We'd done it!

I don't think any of us could see the magnitude of what we had begun. It was like one of the original Mickey Rooney-Judy Garland movies, a group of young kids in a clubhouse saying,

We'll put on a show and everyone will come!

Makeover Italian Style

A fat Italian woman is an oxymoron, certainly in Florence anyway. They are all thin, though they may not think so themselves. They not only fight their own appetites to achieve this but, in my experience, also admonish friends for any signs of extra weight or obvious joy at *indulgence*. One time when I returned from the US having shed a few pounds, we were at an *aperitivo* and I mentioned that I was hungry and should eat something, when a restraining hand was placed on my arm; I was warned that I would *undo all my good work*. In the US if I'd shown any reluctance in partaking what was on offer, I'd have been encouraged with: *eat, you look great!*

I live in LA, so obviously I'm pretty aware of what women are prepared to do in the pursuit of youthful looks and perceived beauty. I'm not a stranger to a *bit of help* myself and in my early days in Florence I was happy to be introduced to the brilliant and kind Dr Georgios Foukis. It went way below his expertise, but he became the man I called to make sure my cold wasn't pneumonia, my gas not a heart attack, my rash not Dutch Elm disease.

Though an eminent plastic surgeon, it wasn't the lure of the knife that drew me to Dr Foukis (he did once perform a small operation on a long-ago scar - I'll spare you the details) but rather some of the less invasive, yet very effective, treatments available at his splendid venture *Skin Aesthetic Clinic*.

Skin, which is located a few steps from the Ponte Vecchio, in the renovated medieval Barbadori Tower, offers the absolute latest and greatest aesthetic techniques. Designed by the renowned architect Michael Young, the clinic is an aesthetic masterpiece itself, featured in many design magazines. It's a luxurious setting in which to relax and be pampered. One of my favorite procedures was, and still is on my return trips to Florence, what I call the *Triple Treat,* involving a facial machine that carries out a photo-facial, a microdermabrasion and a suction technique that stimulates the collagen. The results are immediate and dramatic. I'm also no stranger to *Botox* and filler treatments and have always gotten better results at *Skin* than in the US. As for photo-hair-removal, let's just say I'll never have to shave under my arms again. And, all my visits cost considerably less than anything similar back home.

The good news is that no matter what procedure is done to me at *Skin,* I still look like myself; the bad news is - I still look like myself! I don't have the Joan Rivers *worked-on* look, though alas I'll never likely be taken for Julia Roberts or Nicole Kidman. I always leave *Skin* feeling - and looking like - a rejuvenated version of me. I admire Dr Foukis because he has no hesitation in telling my much younger friends to come back in ten years if they ask for *Botox* or request surgery. Funny, he has never said no to my requests...

Given my attraction to the delights of *Skin,* few people were surprised when I suggested we take a cue from reality shows such as *Extreme Makeover* and *What Not to Wear,* for a column in *The Florentine.* I came up with the idea of the *Ultimate Italian Makeover* for an article and, to test if this would be appealing as a recurring feature, I volunteered myself as the first candidate for transformation.

To this end, I headed off to Centro Benessere on the luxurious Via Tornabuoni with its historic palazzos, exclusive designer shops and elegant bars and cafès. Once I arrived at *Olimpo Gabrio Staff*, Gabrio, owner of the exclusive beauty and hair salon, reminded me upfront that beauty is, of course, only skin deep. His new salon, he informed me, was a place where beauty was treated from head to toe and from inside out, *Prove it!* I challenged him and we set a date for me to spend a day at the mercy of his team for my *Ultimate Italian Makeover.*

At 10.00am the following Friday, I showed up ready for my transformation. Given it was going to be a one-time only experience I was clear with Gabrio that I was strictly after treatments that showed *immediate* and *visible* results. The salon's Japanese and ayurvedic therapies may well improve the balance of my meridians or increase my endorphins and serotonin levels (and I guess this was the *inside* of the *beauty from the inside out* promise) but I was strictly after younger, thinner, and more outwardly beautiful thank you! And besides, inner peace wouldn't make very interesting photographs for *The Florentine* article.

I kicked off with the intriguing concept of a chocolate treatment that promised to exfoliate, improve circulation, and combat cellulite. I quickly undressed to be rubbed, massaged and marinated in a concoction containing the delicious ingredient I'd more usually take pleasure in eating. During the marinade, Moghe, the aesthetician, turned her attention to my face. Sadly, the machine that would take ten years off me wouldn't be available for another three weeks. *I wish.* I had to settle for mere deep cleansing and rejuvenation. This time, a tropical fruit salad that brought together all my favorite gelato flavors - papaya, mango and passion fruit - was applied to my face. My stomach rumbled, driven to action by the delicious aromas of my treatments. I should have eaten more before my visit.

Cleansed of my chocolate and fruit coverings, I was ready for what I really came here for: *the magical thinning machine.* Give me some credit, I never actually *believed* the promise, it was more a wistful holding on to the hope that one day a slim Italian model would pop out of this big-boned American gal. To begin with, my most fatty areas - hips, abdomen and inner thighs - were basted in a sticky paraffin substance. Then I was dressed in a fetching plastic orange suit before being inserted into the *Vibrosauna.* It was a very serious looking piece of equipment; in addition to *having a go* at my excess lipo I was pretty sure it would be able to give me a MRI scan. Once released, I eagerly peered into my suit for signs of escaped and surplus me; the triumph of hope over sanity? I saw only water, and as we know girls, that doesn't count.

A manicure, eyebrow shaping and dyeing, and a pedicure followed. The removal of dry skin from my feet probably accounted for the only permanent weight loss of the day. Then I was ready for my make-up session. I was very pleased with the natural, stylish look I was given, though I wasn't sure I'd be able to replicate it at home. At last it was time for the intervention I knew would have the biggest potential to deliver a transformation in my appearance; I was ready for the true *Italian* hairstyle.

Anna, the colorist, told me what she wanted to do, and having already given up on the hope of finding someone on this side of the ocean with whom I'd feel safe on the hair front, I didn't argue. I put myself entirely in her hands and her foils. To my surprise and delight she created a stunning rich chestnut and blond effect; just the right amount of edge to avoid the *middle-age-patron* look at one extreme and the *freaked-out-punk* look at the other.

Color complete, it was off to the chopping block. Giuseppe didn't consult me about what I wanted done. I'm hardly known for being timid, but I don't think I'd have gotten a word in if I'd tried. Had I found a pause in which to speak I'd have told him that I wanted to keep it long but the scissors were in action before I could attempt any kind of request. I was horrified to see lengths of my precious locks dropping to the floor. *He's an expert, he knows what he's doing,* I talked to myself to calm my rising panic. *And if it doesn't look great, it'll grow back,* I worked out my fall-back position. *Did he just take a gash out of the middle of my scalp?* Whether he did or not I still gasped. Scissor-happy Giuseppe assured me, in broken English,

You must relax, Nita, trust me, it will all be good.

I guess I had no other choice.

The haircut was fabulous. It totally suited me and got rid of hair damaged by past mistakes and harsh treatment. I also felt it would be easy for me to keep it looking that way myself. I was more than happy with both the color and cut.

Hair all sorted, it was onto the last part of the deal. Gabrio had promised to find a clothing shop that would complete my new look with a stunning outfit. I walked out of the salon and down the street where Adelaide, the manager of *Escada*, was waiting for me. By this time it was 7.00pm; it had taken nine hours to get me to look reasonably presentable! I was led downstairs to the salon and given the kind of VIP treatment it would take me no time at all to get used to. I played dress-up while Adelaide brought everything I needed in my size, including shoes and fabulous bags for each outfit. I was pleasantly surprised to find that you don't have to be Kate Moss to shop at *Escada*. Or maybe the Vibrosauna had really worked…

In the end I picked an outfit and we took some photos for *The Florentine*. Alas, I wasn't going to make it out of the front doors with the clothes! But the day wasn't over and, *Escada* black pantsuit or not, I still wanted to get some reaction as to the outcome of my day at the salon…before the results wore off.

The *oohs* and *arhs* of the friends who met me for cocktails were generous. As far as I was concerned, the best verdict was:

Mamma mia Nita, you look so Italian!

La Dolce Vita in Via Ghibellina

By the time the first issue of *The Florentine* had been ready to go to print we hadn't sold all the advertising space. Given that our readers were not Italians, but that most of the would-be advertisers we were trying to connect them with were, we knew we were going to have to seriously prove we'd be reaching a market that would bring them increased business. It was to be a challenging task.

As we'd had the space still available, and were anxious to get the first issue out, we offered our generous writers, who had contributed their efforts without payment, the opportunity to put in free advertisements for any services or businesses with which they had associations. Suzi Jenkins was one of the saintly people who had helped us. Amongst other assistance, she kindly shared a considerable amount of information from a website she'd created for people visiting her in Florence.

Suzi explained that although she didn't personally have any use for our offer, her friend had an apartment that she wanted to rent out and it would be great if she could take out an advertisement on her behalf. I had no hesitation in agreeing and soon received the details: *a three bedroom, three bathroom apartment, in the center, with parking and a garden.* Tony and I wanted to live in the center and having a garage and an outside space of our own would be almost unthinkable luxuries. Amazingly the rent was about what we were already paying for a place considerably less ideal.

We made an appointment with Louise, the owner, to go and see the apartment before the details were published in *The Florentine* (there had to be some perks to running the paper). Very soon Tony, Montana and I found ourselves walking into the most beautiful, hip, place that I'd ever seen in Florence. The ground floor apartment was part of a converted building which had originally been a convent, dating from the 1500s. When Louise and her husband had bought it three years earlier, it had been totally trashed, having been used as an artists' studio and never having been renovated or used as a proper residence. In the *before* pictures, it resembled an indoor junk yard.

For three years the renovation was a major project for Louise. She had turned it into her dream house. Structurally, she closed in bedrooms on the sides of the upper loft so that the main living space had two-storey high ceilings. All of the rooms opened up to a beautiful patio and garden, a treasure to find right in the middle of the city. Louise, who is Danish, had the kitchen cabinets brought in from Denmark. She scrubbed and painted, scouring the markets for the fabrics, furniture and fixtures which went to create the final, stunning effect. She found antique chandeliers at warehouses or flea markets and then painted the metal fittings black or white to give them an original, eclectic look. Antique mirrors covered the massive doors separating the office and kitchen. It was extraordinary. Montana's eyes were huge, and we were all salivating as we imagined ourselves living in this palazzo.

Louise was six months pregnant and glowing. She was delighted at the impact her dream home had on us. Not only did we all fall in love with the apartment that day, we fell in love with Louise! She said she had been *desperata* about what to do with the place. The couple had poured their energy, creativity, sweat and money into it for three years and loved the results of their labor. During the course of this, while living at her in-laws, Louise had had one child and was about to have her second. She explained her confusion: the open stairways and loft configuration wasn't the greatest for babies and her husband traveled a lot too, so they felt safer living in his family home.

Desperate to tell Louise we wanted the place, but trying not to be too pushy about snatching her dream home away from her, I politely enquired,

What kind of work does your husband do?

Oh, he works in his family business…Ferragamo? Her tone far from assumed we'd be familiar with this name.

Ferragamo? I checked I'd heard right, *As in where I've been buying shoes and purses for the last 20 years whenever I can afford them?*

Yes, that would be it, she shyly confirmed.

She explained that when she'd first moved to Italy from Denmark she'd never heard of the *Ferragamo* name so hadn't expected us to know it either. I told Louise that just two days earlier I'd been talking to a friend in California, who'd told me,

Nita, you have to get a picture of the Ferragamo twins on the front page of your paper! I saw an article about them and they are drop-dead gorgeous. You'll sell a million copies!

I asked her if she knew the twins. She laughed out loud, *I'm married to one of them!*

Well, not only was I going to get to live in the most stylish, *ganzo* apartment in Florence, but I'd made a connection with one of Florence's most glamorous families. I would come to know a lot more about these amazing people and the family business that all started with Salvatore Ferragamo designing and making his first pair of shoes at the age of four. He went on to spend time in American, becoming shoemaker to the Hollywood stars and attracting customers such as Marilyn Monroe, Eva Peron and the Maharani of Cooch Behar. When he died in 1960 his wife Wanda and their children continued to build the *Ferragamo* brand until it achieved the global prominence it has today, adding bags, eyewear, silk accessories, watches, perfumes and a ready-to-wear clothes line to its flagship footwear.

While I never got the twins on the front page of *The Florentine,* I did get to interview Jamie's brother, Salvatore, and their father Ferruccio. However, the friendship I developed with both Louise and Jamie has been the source of more fun, love, adventure and kindness than I could ever have hoped to discover. Well yes, OK, I admit it, the source of a few fantastic scarves, boots and purses too...

Nita Tucker's Top Ten List of Things You Need to Know

…that Italians assume you already *do* know, *should* know and are stupid for *not* knowing!

#10: The Price of un Caffé
If you drink your cappuccino at the bar, it costs €1; if you drink it while sitting at a table (even if you bought it at the bar) it costs more, usually double; if you choose one of the more refined places like in Piazza Signoria or Piazza della Republica, what you end up paying for one cappuccino, should, at the very least, entitle you to take the table home.

#9: A Queue by Any Other Name Will Not Be Formed
Italians aren't interested in lines, unlike the English, who will queue up in their own home to sit down to dinner. Americans are known to occasionally push, shove and *cut in line*. In Italy, there's not even acknowledgment that a line of any kind exists, much less respect for, or adherence to it.

My first week in the supermarket, at the check-out, a short, older woman just places her cart in front of me, and out of respect for the elderly, I allowed it. No thanks, no sign of appreciation. When I ask Catia about this often repeated and annoying experience, and the irritating sense of entitlement these women display, Catia suggests maybe it's because they've gone through two wars and have just had to take care of themselves, doing whatever was necessary to survive. But she admitted that this didn't really explain the same thing frequently happening to her, only with much younger people.

Along the same lines, if, when driving, Italians see an opening in the road, they go for it; to do anything else would be wasteful and stupid. What I view as rude and disorderly, the Italians, it seems, think of as just practical, common sense.

#8: That the Church and State are Separate

While the Italian and US governments are both, in principle secular, it surprised me to find although Italy is 95% Catholic, in nearly every way there is a much clearer separation of Church and State than in the US. My first month in Florence, I mentioned to Catia,

Most of my friends only have one or two children, not like here.

She looked at me, puzzled,

Nita, Italy has the lowest birthrate of any country in the world, about 1.2 children per family. In fact, we have a concern that the Italian population is disappearing!

I explained to Catia, when I grew up, if there was a family with 4 or more kids in the neighborhood, they were *always* Catholic. I probed,

But you're Catholic, no birth control, no abortions, right?

We're Catholic, Nita, but we're not stupid. Why would you have children if you can't afford to take care of them properly?

But Catia, the Church? The Pope? We're in Italy!

Nita, have you noticed the cigarette machines on the streets, all over Florence, outside of the buildings? Well, next to these are vending machines selling condoms, birth control available 24 hours a day.

The following year, over dinner at my friend's house, several women (me as the only non-Italian) were talking about the merits of having sex before marriage. My wonderfully opinionated friend, Silvia, stated that,

Of course you should have sex beforehand, or how would you know what good sex is like? And, not to mention the horror of marrying someone who you didn't like in bed! My daughter is only 11, but for sure I'll tell her to have sex before she marries someone.

I had to point out,

...but Silvia, you send your daughter to a Catholic school. The nuns are telling her the opposite.

By then, I was used to the withering look Silvia, and many others before and after, gave to me; the look that said how naïve and stupid Americans are!

Nita, the nuns know better than that, and even if they do say something, Lucia isn't going to listen to a nun about relationship matters.

So yes, birth control is easily found and prescribed in Italy and abortions are available through National Healthcare.

Another topic that frequently pops up during religious and political debate in the US is homosexuality, both openly acknowledged and widely accepted in Italy. At a personal level, the striking thing is, that there seems to be little inner conflict for Catholics with being homosexual (or using birth control or having an abortion - all outlawed by the Catholic Church) and following their religion, including attending Church and taking communion. Also, whereas in the US politicians and even business executives are fearful of openly supporting practices or lifestyles outlawed by the Church, in Italy, they do not see that others should feel shame or attempt to conceal who they are or what they do, in any way.

#7: Taxis - What Happened to Your Fare?

You watch the fare and get your money out as you drive up to your destination; you look up and the meter reads €8.95 and then with a sudden push of a button, the fare is now €11.50. This occurs the world over, but the reasons for the increase in Italy are so cryptically varied: a) you called the taxi, which is an added charge or b) it's after 10.00pm or 11.00pm at night, or a different time, depending on the season, day of the week, and whether you are a woman or man or c) you have gone to, or are coming from, the airport or train station or d) a new tariff applies or e) all of the above.

#6: Opening Hours - The Rule is: *There is No Rule*

...but some of the following customs may, or may not, apply. On Mondays, many stores are either closed or don't open until after 2:30pm. Restaurants often close on Mondays, or Tuesdays, and some close for dinner or just for lunch. One of my favorite places to eat dinner is closed only on Saturday evenings. Some stores, usually those in the center, have continual hours, meaning they don't close for the afternoon *pausa*. The ones that do close re-open at 4:00pm or 4:30pm or 5:30pm, or never. The last place to try and find out an opening time is the sign on a shop or business' door; the signs are there but the spaces in which to write the times are usually left frustratingly blank.

The same uncertainty holds for Sunday opening times. The supermarkets are usually closed on Sundays, except that is, for the last Sunday of the month. And whatever anyone tells you about an opening time, no matter if it is contained in a government decree or is posted on an official website and it's the word of the mayor or even the owner of the store, you can always add to their words...*except not always.*

Regarding museums, I eventually concluded that the imagination once used to create the amazing art housed inside them, is now applied to scheduling the opening hours. A xeroxed sign at the Medici Chapel, a much-visited state museum, read something like this,

Open every 3rd Monday in summer from 11.30am-1:30pm except for August; Tuesdays and Thursdays from 9.00am to 5.00pm; Friday afternoons in winter and weekends have different hours every second weekend depending on when the Uffizi is open.

I checked that someone hadn't put it up for a joke, but no.

#5: Finding an Address
In Florence, addresses follow the standard even numbers on one side of the street, odd on the other, again… *except not always.* There is the matter of the *rosso* or red numbers. In times past, red numbers were used for residential as opposed to business addresses. Now no such distinction is made, but existing numbers e.g. 32r, the *r* being for *rosso*, remain. And of course, these red numbers have very little to do sequentially with the black numbers. In your search for 32r, you might pass a black 30 and a black 34, and often even a black 32, only for you to arrive at a hotel when you are looking for a bike repair shop. The place you are *actually* looking for may be two blocks further up next to a black 58.

#4: The Enigma of Signage
If you are driving to Siena from Florence, you follow signs that take you to a roundabout. You look for the exit for Siena to find that 5 out of the 6 exits say Siena. I have no advice on what to do if you find yourself faced with such a situation and needing to make a choice. After many years, I have yet to figure out how to follow the signs to get

somewhere. The Italians themselves, I've observed, have no issue with their signage at all.

#3: Getting on the Right Train

You are in Florence; you want to go to the famous antique market in Arezzo, which happens the first weekend of the month. You go to the train station and buy a ticket to Arezzo. You are given a ticket that says *Arezzo* along with the train number and the departure time. You look at the reader board to see from which track or *binario* your train is leaving. Arezzo is not on the board. Rome is on the board, Milano is on the board, Palermo is on the board, but no Arezzo. You look at your number to see if it matches one of the major destinations, but there are no numbers except departure times on the board. Then of course you try to match up the time, but both the trains for Milano and Roma leave at the same time so you're still not sure. Finally, you ask a train company employee, who looks at your ticket, the reader board, and then at you, because he can't believe he's met such an idiot. Then, he scolds you for wasting his time on such a ridiculous question, because *obviously you take the train to Roma - you imbecile!*

#2: When to Tip

Wait staff in Italy get paid wages and do not depend on tips. There's also a charge, called *coperta* which is added to the check for water, bread and service. Still tipping is appreciated; it just doesn't have to be a percentage of the bill, but more based on the quality of the service and work done. Most taxi drivers do not expect tips, but again, it doesn't hurt to be generous and kind.

#1: Asking For a Discount

The number one thing you need to know, that *every* Italian knows, and thinks you're *stupid* for not knowing is that you can always and anywhere ask for a discount. Whether in a designer store or buying fruit in the market, asking for *uno sconto* is an acceptable, even expected request. You don't ask for it like you're getting ready to drive a tough bargain, more with a friendly tone of enquiry. Your request will be met in the same good natured spirit. Enjoy!

Non ci Posso Credere! Is there Nothing Sacred?

Another day and another perk, a coveted invitation to visit the medieval town of Pietrasanta and the marble quarries of Carrara in the company of the patrons of Syracuse University of Florence, and Professor Rab Hatfield, one of the foremost experts on Michelangelo. I'd driven around the mountains of Carrara before, north-west of Florence; they are dramatic, quite stunning. It's difficult to believe that you are not looking at snow-capped peaks and glaciers, but rather the white of the marble from which so many of the world's treasures have been created. The Pantheon and Trajan's Column in Rome; Michelangelo's *David;* the Duomo di Siena and even *the* Marble Arch in London all started off in the mountains and caves of this beautiful region.

At Pietrasanta, where the cobbled streets are lined with artists' studios, artisan workshops, cafés, trattorias and shops selling antiques and high end fashion, Rab took us to meet the eccentric Brit, John Taylor. An internationally renowned sculptor, he came to Italy in 1990 after winning the *Prix de Rome*, a scholarship given by the British School of Rome; he never went home. Delightfully irreverent in the hallowed surroundings, John was roughly dressed and plainly spoken while being very charming at the same time. He lives and works with the marble, as well as teaching sculpture in Pietrasanta and Florence. Our tour commenced with a visit to the little Renaissance church and the extraordinary frescoes created by Fernando Botero, a contemporary Columbian sculptor and familiar face in the town sometimes referred to as the *City of the Artists* or *Small Athens.*

After the church, we headed to the workshop where John and several other sculptors work the marble. It was fascinating to see the tools, methods and the magnitude of the skill and effort required to chisel the rock to reveal the artist's vision and the true beauty of the material. John and his associates sculpt under a co-operative arrangement. Their workshop is owned by the Barsanti family, themselves once great sculptors. The compound has been in existence since the 18th century. Now the family rents out studios and sources and sells antique marbles, primarily for restoration and repairs, as well as selling completed sculptures which they display in a garden.

We took a walk outside and viewed some of the replicas of famous Italian classics, including a Donatello *David* and a number of Roman soldiers that were available to purchase. I was completely taken aback to learn that these were not carved in Italy, but in China! And to provide evidence of what was, to me, quite a shocking revelation, John drew our attention to a number of details including the more Chinese appearance of *David's* stomach, not saggy exactly, but distinctly less muscular than the original. He also pointed out the stoic expressions of the Roman soldiers which seemed to have much more in common with the faces of the warriors of the famous terracotta army uncovered in Shaanxi province in China, than with any more local, long ago, centurions.

Non ci posso credere! Unbelievable - is there nothing sacred?

I asked why these iconic Italian forms were made in China *and* with Chinese marble, given the materials and skills that existed right where we stood,

Isn't it a little like bringing coal to Newcastle?

I should have anticipated the answer, basically, for the same reason many of the designer clothes and textiles are made there today…because it's cheaper. In the case of these Chinese-Italian statues you could have three for the price of one 100% Italian one.

Not with sculpture so much, but in the fashion and textile industries this situation has been much talked about in terms of its impact on the legacy of Italy's contribution in these areas and, of course, the economic and social effects of the trend. Since many Italian designers are having their clothes and accessories made in China, India and Eastern Europe, there is much concern about protecting and promoting the *Made in Italy* label, traditionally associated with stylish and quality leather goods. Of course, the most significant result of more imported goods is the loss of Italian jobs by the thousands; the kinds of jobs, in the case of the leather industry, that Italians assumed would never leave the country.

And now it appeared that even the creation of a *Donatello* could be outsourced!

After Pietrasanta, we headed to Carrara. I'd never actually seen marble excavated before and was thrilled we'd be visiting the Fantiscritti quarry, so named because of the primitive, and therefore considered infant-like, writings that were found there. We were given a tour by Francesca, whose family owns the marble concession inside the mountain. She took us, by shuttle, into its depths, until we arrived at the center of an immense cave much, much larger than the massive interior of Il Duomo. This is the source of most of the Carrara white marble of which I learned there are two grades. The type found inside the cave is hard, compressed, heavy and used for buildings, floors, and kitchen counter-tops. It's not traditionally used for sculpting although some contemporary sculptors now do so. The second type is known as statuary marble, a much purer white form, found in the outside quarries rather than deep within the mountain, and most commonly used for creating works of art. Marble is made of calcite, a form of calcium carbonate, and somehow what was now marble, on the inside of the caves and on the outside of the mountains, had been, a seriously long time ago, the ocean floor!

It was fascinating to see how the huge blocks were cut from the sides of the massive cave and then tested to see if they were solid. The latter is done by striking them with a hammer (the size of something you'd use to pound in a small nail), to see if the sound traveled to the other side of it. If there's a crack, no echo emerges and the block is deemed unusable for a large piece of work.

From the cave, we drove around to the other side of the mountain to visit Ravacione, the outside quarry where Michelangelo is said to have obtained the marble from which he created his exquisite masterpieces. I don't suppose, for one moment, he'd ever have imagined that, one day in the future, his fellow Italians would be importing replicas of his own works…from China!

Losing My Virginity

I was very excited that Marco and I had been able to get press passes to meet Sir Richard Branson when he came to Florence to promote the *Virgin Unite Charity Concert* and to celebrate the opening of a new *Virgin Active Health Club* on the city's southern outskirts. Besides the thrill of getting to meet an international celebrity, it was rewarding to know we'd enjoy the status of other newspapers in Florence, a new treat for *The Florentine*. Given the way these things work in Italy, it was a series of personal connections, Marco's and mine, which had secured us the right to join the press corps wanting to get up close and personal with the then 55 year-old entrepreneur. At the time the *Virgin* brand was splashed across 200 companies, in 30 countries, enjoying a particularly high profile within the music, finance and airline industries.

After showing a short video about the work of his charitable foundation, for which the up-coming concert would raise awareness and funds, the casually dressed, almost rumpled Branson, invited questions from the audience. Not one to be held back by my lack of experience or familiarity with protocol, I was the only one who shot up my hand,

I'm Nita Tucker, from *The Florentine*!

I asked, given his enormous wealth and resources, and thus pretty much the option to do anything in the world, how he chose what to do next, which business or which charity to take on and into which to invest his time, energy and money.

I loved his answer, not least of all because it resonated with me personally. He said his first career was as a journalist, and he chose it because he wanted to make a difference in some way. His biggest driver, in whatever he did, continued to be a desire to make a positive impact on the world.

Branson's version and scale of making a difference is backed by his belief that wealth comes with responsibility. His business ventures have shaken up a number of industries, his services and pricing challenging competitors to get their act together and offer a better deal to the customer, the airlines being the most dramatic example of this. Branson talked about his approach as,

Challenging the conglomerates and keeping them honest. For example, I think we did that with Virgin Air and that now, British Airways and other airlines are better companies because of it.

Telling the rapt audience more about his foundation's charitable works', he explained that it was all about looking at *what needed to get handled* in the world. He saw AIDS and malaria prevention and treatment as two significant sectors where immediate action was critical and the drugs and education to help already available. The opportunity, right now, was to use grass-root organizations to get these essentials directly to those who need them most.

Answering questions from other journalists, Branson outlined how some of his ventures straddled both a business opportunity and a *need to get handled* issue. He talked a little about *Virgin Fuels* which was aiming to develop a viable and profitable, non-polluting energy source to reduce dependence on the OPEC countries and to tackle climate change. *Doing everything better and doing some things differently,* was how he summed up his overall strategy.

I was impressed by Branson's considered responses to our questions; there was nothing slick or practiced about them. This struck me further when I had the opportunity to interview him in a more intimate setting, the hot-tub room of the gym, though alas not actually in the hot tub! The press was taken in to meet him in groups of three. My trio consisted of a reporter from NBC, one from MTV - and me! I kept waiting for someone to find out that I had snuck in, to reveal that I had no credentials or fake ones (I had been known to do this in my youth). But no, I realized, I actually belonged here, I was being taken seriously, I was the editor-in-chief of *The Florentine!*

This fascinating man answered more questions about his foundation's work and then one of the reporters asked about his leadership style. He quietly gave himself credit for the way in which he was able to inspire others to come together and do great things. He shared his own need to combine hard work with plenty of fun and was clearly excited with the *Virgin Galactic* venture which would, before too many years, he was certain, be taking passengers, himself included, into space. (As I write, the reality gets very close - around $200,000 will secure you a ticket.)

When asked about the mark he'd like to leave on the world he replied,

For more young people to live who wouldn't be there if we hadn't had assisted.

A lot of big things about Sir Richard Branson impressed me that day, one of them being that he didn't, like many wealthy individuals, have his *pet* or *vanity* cause, and looked not at what he wanted or liked to do, but at what was wanted and needed in the world. But, in the end, it was a very small thing that stuck in my mind and gave me another insight into the way the man operates. It happened when the PR person handling the press walked into the room to rotate one of the reporters out, his turn being over. Branson, who certainly wasn't having the time of his life stuffed into a tiny hot tub room answering much asked questions, could have easily just let her get on with her job. But, instead, he stopped her, saying that the reporter had only had the chance to ask one question. Somehow, the fact that he'd noticed this, and acted on it, struck me as very decent.

I couldn't wait to share my press conference experience with the readers of *The Florentine*. I hoped they too would be energized by some insights into this incredible man and his approach to life, business and charity, and that they would be moved to support his foundation. On the way back to the office, I was left with the sense of having just been in the presence of one of the great humanitarians of our time.

Marco, it turned out, was left with a very different impression of Sir Richard Branson (and one that was probably shared by many of the other well-heeled Italians at the event),

His clothes were all wrinkled! He looked like he'd slept in them on the airplane over to Italy and, incredibly, not even thought to get changed!

La bella figura blindsides me again.

Hanging with the Thespians

One evening, I was invited to dinner by my beautiful, bright and sophisticated friend, Ellyn Toscano, a lawyer, former aid to a NYC congressman and then director at Villa La Pietra, the venue for NYU's study-abroad program in Florence. The other guests would all be associated with a play, *The Giant*. The cast and company, including director, costumer and writer were to be guests at the Villa to rehearse, edit, and perform a reading of the play before its opening in the West End in London. Needless to say, star-gazer that I am, I accepted the invitation with much anticipation. About 12 of us gathered at a long table in a restaurant near Piazza Sant' Ambrogia.

The Giant is about the making of Michelangelo's *David*. As described in the play-bill: *it is historical fiction, lots of facts and truths with a heap of speculation and creative license thrown in*. It tells the story surrounding the transformation of the large slab of marble into Michelangelo's masterpiece. The main characters are the great sculptor himself; his contemporary and portrayed as a rival, Leonardo da Vinci; and Vito, the 18 year-old quarryman who is chosen to model for the *David* and with whom both great artists are seen to develop an obsession.

The Giant's playwright, Sir Anthony Sher, is a much accomplished and lauded actor and writer, knighted for his contributions to the theatre. He has written plays, memoirs and novels and has enjoyed an illustrious acting career. His breakthrough happened in 1984 when he played Richard III for the Royal Shakespeare Company, receiving his first *Laurence Olivier Award*. On the personal side, he is noteworthy because he and his partner, Greg Doran, producer of *The Giant*, were the first gay couple to form a civil partnership in England; and then the first such couple to be invited to spend the weekend at Sandringham as guests of Prince Charles and Camilla Parker Bowles.

Also at the gathering was John Light, the British actor playing Michelangelo. Obviously a noted actor in his own right, I admit the wow for me was that he was married to the Canadian actress Neve Campbell (though I've read they are now divorced). Leonardo was played by Roger Allam, another of Ellyn's guests and *Laurence Olivier Award* winner. One of his many acting credits includes playing the role of the private secretary, alongside Helen Mirren, in the movie *The Queen*. He's widely known to British TV audiences for playing the part of MP Peter Mannion in series *The Thick of It*. Besides being (in his words) *too tired, too old, and too talented*, he speaks several languages, has the sharpest wit, and is incredibly sexy.

At what a lofty table I found myself seated!

Of course I was intrigued to meet *David* himself and knew that Stephen Hagen who was taking this role, was a name to look out for, a superstar in the making. Stephen has such a keen likeness to Michelangelo's creation that when the troupe went to Carrara, the original source of the marble from which it was carved, people were pointing at him in the streets. He's a magnificent hunk; tall, exquisite, funny, sweet and most definitely heterosexual and I know the latter, because I asked him. He was amused when I told him that my rule of thumb, developed during ten years living in San Francisco, was to assume any man 75% or more good-looking was gay. My system *usually* worked; but this young man from Northern Ireland had just blown it! During the reading of *The Giant* the following Friday, there was a time when Michelangelo tells his *David* to take off his shirt. Since it was just a read through, Stephen just made a motion to indicate his disrobing. *Damn!* I hear from the student sitting behind me, giving voice to all our thoughts…

For Love or Money

It was our intention to make *The Florentine* into a commercially viable operation. Both being experienced in business, Tony and I also hoped that, having identified a niche that obviously needed to be filled, perhaps we would even achieve some considerable success with the project. I have to admit, we had conversations about grandeur and wealth, about becoming newspaper magnates and taking this idea to other Italian cities. And why stop at Italy?

When we arrived in Florence we certainly weren't wealthy but we were relatively debt free. Given our unexpected windfall we'd calculated we'd have enough savings to get us through two or three years. I was still working as an independent consultant and despite my earnings being unpredictable, was confident they'd pull us through. After being in Italy for six months, we sold our house in Santa Fe and although most of the proceeds went back to the bank, we got our hands on a modest sum for the sale. The hope was that we'd arrive back in the US at some unknown date in the future with, at the very least, a down payment on a small condo or home. Overall, we thought we were more or less set to live comfortably in Florence.

When we decided to go ahead with making the idea of the newspaper into the reality of *The Florentine* we knew that there'd be some upfront costs: paying a managing editor, the fee for the *Director Responsible* and printing charges, were some of the more significant out-lays amongst a number of other unavoidable expenses. The plan was, once off the ground, we'd start to build the advertising revenue that would begin to cover on-going costs and eventually turn a profit.

Our Italian partners' immediate financial expectations were not so much that *The Florentine* would provide them with direct income. Rather, they saw the paper attracting work from advertisers using their graphic design business to do the ad lay-outs. In addition, they would be able to promote their business, and Leo his portrait service, in the paper. They looked to *The Florentine* for exposure rather than income.

None of us had money to make a capital investment into this venture; it had to be a more of a *pay-as-you-go* situation. Most of the hard costs came from Tony's and my pocket, but the majority of the normal start-up expenses were allayed because our partners already had the necessities required to run a business: the office, computers, printers, copiers, phones and the legal licenses.

In the early days, we thought it would be a no-brainer to sell advertising. Florence is one of the world's top tourist destinations. An overwhelming majority of its visitors read English, either as a first or second language, and only a very small amount of this influx of guests speak Italian. The paper was the one and only consistent source of news - in English - in Florence. With seemingly no competition, we had the market cornered. If Italian businesses wanted to market their services to this substantial number of tourists and expats, they would clearly see the sense in placing advertisements with *The Florentine*...right?

Wrong! I've been a management consultant for over 30 years. I'm paid large sums of money to give advice to leaders in multinational corporations. I have a stellar track record of delivering results that lead to increased productivity and profitability. Yet none of the wisdom, insight and experience I've gained along the way applied to doing business in Italy - none of it - nada, nulla, niente, zilch!

It didn't take Tony and I long to recall the warnings of friends that the chances of us creating a profitable venture with the newspaper were less than slim, especially given that even established newspapers in the US were either fighting off, or actually experiencing, bankruptcy and closure.

What we hadn't taken into account was that, for Italians, when it came to promoting their business, it was vital to them that their friends, family and competitors see their promotional efforts. *Looking good* in the eyes the people they knew, was of even greater importance to these businesses than the extra revenue advertising could bring them. This meant that they would choose to promote their goods and services in Italian newspapers such as *La Republica*, totally irrespective of whether or not the newspaper's readership was made up of the customers they were aiming to attract. Similarly perplexing, a hair salon was opening on Via Tornabuoni and the owner told me that his target clientele would mainly consist of wealthy Americans, the very reason he thought I should write an article about his salon. He shared that he didn't have money for advertising. However, he then proceeded to spend €300,000 on an opening party, an event to which he didn't invite a single English speaker!

The enigma was that while *The Florentine* was clearly not a commercial winner, in terms of the goals it set out to achieve of providing Italian news in English, and making a positive difference to ex-pats and tourists' experience of their time in Florence, it quickly became a massive success. The newspaper had so clearly filled a gap and we'd achieved our initial vision. The feedback we received that first year was overwhelmingly gratifying for everyone working on *The Florentine*. Ex-pats told us about trips they'd taken because of articles they'd read. The British and American Counsel let us know how grateful they were that they had, at last, a way to communicate important information to their target audience, with similar sentiments expressed by the *Comune* and the *Region*. English language teachers told us what a great aid to learning the paper was - even the president of the *Region*, when I met him, reported that his English teacher used *The Florentine* as his textbook. People at exhibitions, or concerts, or religious services said they'd found out about the events from the paper, maybe from a copy they'd picked up in their hotel. Even Italians thanked us for the clarity of these pages, now their own source of events information given the quirky and complex way the Italian papers captured these details.

It was terribly frustrating to see how *The Florentine* was such a huge success at one level, while at the same time struggling to operate as a viable commercial venture. As well as struggling to cover the costs of the paper, let alone make a profit, Tony and I discovered an additional challenge to our personal financial situation: the error of our calculations when it came to the cost of living in Florence. Basically, it proved much more expensive than we had expected. The money we thought would last for at least two years, disappeared, almost before our eyes, in just ten months. And, significantly, I'd resigned from my consulting work after four months in Italy. The paper had flirted with me, pulled me in and stolen my heart. I could see not only that I was needed but that I provided the 'spark' and was critical to driving the content of the paper that the readers of our 10,000 print run so loved, and upon which they were now depending.

Tony saw the writing on the wall pretty quickly when it came to the prospect of *The Florentine* providing any kind of income for us and the subsequent impact of this on our seriously dwindling bank balance. Also, Tony, being a businessman, found no satisfaction working on, and investing in, a venture that clearly wasn't going to make any money.

He wanted to return to the US.

I wanted to stay in Italy.

We talked, cried, argued, and after one year in Florence, both agreed that *he* would go back to the US and find a livelihood to support our family. *I*, on the other hand, would remain in Italy with Montana and the fledgling *Florentine*. The decision to stay was easy - I loved the newspaper, my work and Florence. Saying goodbye to Tony on the other hand was extremely painful; I loved him too, very much.

The day he left to go back to the US was a grey one for us both.

It's News to Me!

In the early days Tony and I worked together to find people to write feature articles and placed a *want ad* on an incredibly useful website serving many cities around the world, called the *English Yellow Pages*. We asked for mother-tongue English speakers, to *volunteer* to write for the paper. Having no idea what response to expect, we were delighted to receive dozens of submissions including some from experienced professional writers that thought the paper was a brilliant or worthy idea. Calling for volunteers, we thought, would be a temporary stop-gap until we were in a position to offer payment. As it turned out, currencies other than cash have continued to bring most of *The Florentine* articles into print. Fortunately for us and our readers, a love of Florence and Italy and all things Italian, and a desire to share this passion, seems to have been quite enough motivation for the kind and talented writers who submitted articles to the newspaper over the years. And given the financial challenges of the paper, this proved to be a significant blessing.

Of course, we were working it out as we went, but over time we learned some critical lessons that helped us to define the editorial line that would become my own responsibility to follow as editor-in-chief. The first lesson learned was the need to aim the content of *The Florentine* to the resident ex-pats rather than the tourists, even though the 50,000 or so of the former was tiny compared to the million plus a year of the latter. If we aimed the articles more towards tourists, the English speaking residents declared the content garbage. However, if we geared the paper to the residents' needs and interests, the tourists ironically seemed to like it more too. I guess it went back to what was missing for me and Tony when he came up with the need for a paper like *The Florentine* in the first place. There was something about reading and feeling a part of what was happening around you - as a local, an insider, a *belonger*. When I'm in New York, I want to read the *New York Times*, not some *I Love New York* tourist-rag.

The second lesson learned along the way, was that we should only report news not already available in English. This meant that we didn't cover international news because the *International Herald Tribune* was already available and would always be the better source of information about world events. We did, however cover the local and regional news of Florence and Tuscany as well as the national Italian news. We were aiming to provide something that was not available elsewhere, basically, *Italian news in English*.

Thirdly, we learned to stay away from covering what was considered *ex-pat news* such as articles about what ex-pats were doing in Florence and their get-togethers. The aim of the paper was to make it easier for readers to access Florence and Italy and to enjoy and participate in *Italian* life. *The Florentine* was never created to promote ex-pat networking in a way that would encourage the development of a separate community. Of course, we announced meetings and events in our listings pages but we didn't report on them or feature related articles.

It was what I came to think of as my *truing principle* that became the most critical factor in deciding what made it into the paper - or not. I'd always ask myself, article in hand: *will this make a person's time in Italy more interesting, fulfilling, richer and easier?* I challenged myself to work out how the content of *The Florentine* could achieve this end. How could we give readers greater access to the life, history, culture and art of this beautiful place in such a way as to build on the appreciation that had drawn them here in the first place? When it came down to it, what seemed to work, as we discovered by trial and error, was that if a topic or story interested *me*, it proved to be of interest to our *readers*. It was extremely convenient that I happened to be so representative of the target market!

Sniffing out and doing the legwork to uncover new and interesting details, facts, people and places served to ensure I was not personally disappointed in my own experience of life in Florence *and* provided the kind of copy I wanted to share with *The Florentine's* readers. The more I began to find out about the city where I now lived, the more fascinated I became, and the thirstier I was for new knowledge and discoveries. My intrigue was equal whether seeking the story behind a particular building such as the one with the beautiful *graffiti* which I regularly rode past on my bike (I'd learn it was this place from which the word *graffiti* came); exploring the significance of the many local and national traditions; discovering the rich and complex history of philosophy, politics and art; or enjoying the latest glamour, glitz and news of the high profile Italian and Florentine families, businesses, politicians and celebrities.

Early on, I learned that what Marco and I would deem to be interesting, enlightening and newsworthy were to be two very different things. For example, I wanted to include an article about why, when all the other bridges in Florence had been bombed in WWII, the iconic Ponte Vecchio had survived. I was fascinated by the story that this was either because Hitler himself, or perhaps his soldiers, thought it was too beautiful to destroy and just couldn't go through with it. I thought the readers would be as intrigued as I was. This was typical of the content about which Marco and I would clash. He declared it boring and, even worse in his eyes, *old news.* It was an impossible struggle to explain that yes, it may be boring and old news *to him,* but that as he wasn't our target reader this was of no consequence whatsoever!

On one level, Italians know that most visitors to their country don't speak or read Italian. Yet, they still seem to think that since all Italians read Italian newspapers every day, then somehow everyone else who is visiting, or especially living in Italy, is reading the same news as them. When I would choose a news or feature story for the paper, Marco would attack my *rotten* selection,

It's been in the papers for a week already Nita, are you crazy? It's not fresh -you're going to kill the newspaper!

If I dared to reply that it may well have been in the *Italian* newspapers for the last week but that *I* didn't know about it he'd get even more rabid,

How do you think you can run a newspaper without knowing the news!

We were both quite certain of our own logic. This difference of opinion persisted with equal amounts of passion displayed by both parties and was the source of endless arguments.

Still, I chose to trust myself on this matter and risked the humiliation and embarrassment that would be heaped upon me, my partners and *The Florentine* as a result of my editorial choices! Early rave reviews from the readers gave me great comfort and I got plenty of confirmation that things were on the right track. Often people's favorable response to the newspaper showed up in offers to contribute content. Once again, the subject matter of their input was a source of conflict between Marco and me.

I remember one time, when a woman who worked for ABC News in Rome contacted me to say that she loved what we were doing and wanted to offer her support by writing something new, or allowing us to reprint some of her past articles. She sent me several captivating pieces but the one which quickly grabbed my attention was about the souvenir vendors who sell religious themed wares around the Vatican. I learned, to my complete surprise, that they are all Jewish, and that this particular market is one the Jews have cornered for decades. I just had to put this well-written and revelatory article into the paper and I went ahead and did just that. Marco thought I was completely insane! To him this was as newsworthy as announcing that the Pope was a Catholic.

Hunt for Red November

Il Borro is a medieval hamlet once owned by the royal family of Italy, the Savoys. The Ferragamo family purchased it from the Savoy heirs in the early '90s. Salvatore, my friend Jamie's twin, named for their grandfather, manages the estate for his father, Ferruccio, and has undertaken a large-scale and highly successful village restoration project. Salvatore has overseen the renovation of every home, apartment, church, stable, cantina, vineyard and villa. The main villa, which was restored by his mother (who also wrote a book about this undertaking), took 7 years of painstaking, detailed artistry to remodel. It now has over 12 bedrooms, each with its own bathroom and all decorated with exquisite furniture, linens, and antique accessories. Throughout the villa, taste and elegance seamlessly combine with modern plumbing, technology and convenience. The outdoor spaces of Il Borro are similarly magnificent. There are beautiful gardens; fields for polo playing; acres of land on which to hunt; and, allowing Salvatore to follow his passion for winemaking, rows and rows of vines producing commercially successful and well-respected vintages bearing the estate's own label.

For luxury vacationers, the apartments, or even the main villa, can be rented. Companies (granted those for whom times are good), can hold meetings, conferences and retreats at Il Borro. My own good fortune to spend many weekends at this wonderful place came through the kind invitations of my friends Louise and Jamie Ferragamo. One of the particularly special reasons for an invite to Il Borro is their annual hunt party which usually takes place in November. For many years now, the couple has taken occupation of the village to gather their friends from different corners of the world to spend the weekend with them, joining in a pheasant hunt and attending a spectacular ball.

The event kicks off on the Friday night with cars arriving from Florence; a private jet from Dubai; flights from London; trains from Switzerland; one guest arrives in his private helicopter! Louise and Jamie's family and friends are a delightful mix that reflects their cultural backgrounds, the places they were schooled, and the venues of their frequent travels. Many of the guests come from Europe, in particular England and Denmark. I'm usually the only one who hails from the US. On that first evening, everyone catches up for dinner at the restaurant in the village.

Saturday morning, those who have actually come to hunt are up early including the late arrivals whose heads have not long hit the pillow. Of course, early in Italy is 8:30am; in the US hunting and fishing would more likely begin sometime around 4.30am. We meet in the dining room of the main villa for un caffé, *cornetto* (croissant), cheese, sausage or anything you want the cooks to make for you. It was always a dream, growing up, to one day experience the luxury of food cooked to order at home! Then we pack up and go over to a neighboring estate, owned by a Count who allows commercial hunts on his centuries old estate, which produces wine and extraordinary olive oil. He has a fairytale domain including several beautiful palazzos, formal gardens and extensive stables. Some of the buildings are over 800 years old. Upon arrival and greetings, we sit down to another meal. And yes, we still haven't been hunting!

Using china, sterling silver and crystal goblets we enjoy bread, sausage, cheese, and fruit. The biggest treat is the sensational olive oil that comes from a crop picked and pressed just days before. The distinct, peppery taste of this *olio nuovo* is indescribable, I couldn't do it justice. The flavor only lasts for a month (after we had our first taste of *olio nuovo* our first November in Florence, Tony, Montana and I were known to have entire meals of just bread dipped in this *liquid gold*).

Then, at last, it's time to pursue the pheasant. I usually find I'm one of a small handful of women amongst 30 or 40 men. No desire to actually shoot anything myself, I enjoy moving around, talking to a number of the always hand-some, often entertaining hunters. And they seem happy enough to have a groupie, old and married though I am. Given that the majority of the women who come to the weekend at Il Borro are 20 or more years younger than me, better dressed, more beautiful and thinner, the hunt is maybe the only time when the odds are in my favor!

Mid-morning, after two sessions of shooting we stop for tea; servers have set up everything including a fire and a grill. We enjoy a spread of bread, cheese, cured meats, the *olio nuovo* and a hot beef broth spiked with wine that exactly hits the spot on a chilly November morning. Stories of early successes and near misses are exchanged and jokes told and fun made; camaraderie with a touch of healthy competition. Then it's off to two more stations in search of the pheasant. And next, you've guessed it, lunch. This time, we eat in one of the ancient buildings on the Count's estate.

It is at least a late lunch, around 3.00pm, and we walk up a set of stairs, remove our muddy boots before entering the dining room of a hunting lodge. The tables are set with the Count's personal china, crest and all. Sofas surround a stone fireplace with a roaring fire. It's crowded but warm and cozy.

The meal is pasta with wild boar sauce, grilled chicken, salad, vegetables; all served while the wine flows and followed by just-baked pastries. Despite the earlier food, the fresh air makes us ravenous and no one holds back.

The women who've opted out of the hunt and stayed back at Il Borro are not short of diversions. They can rest; use the spa and have a massage; go shopping at the famous outlet stores about a 20 minute drive away; horse-back ride; or help Louise set up for the evening party. Whatever their choice, along with the men returned from the hunt, by 5.00pm they'll be back in their rooms getting ready for the evening. Each year there's a different theme for Louise and Jamie's hunt ball. It is expected that you come in costume and everyone does. The children also dress up and while they don't attend the big party, they join the adults as they enjoy their cocktails in the main villa beforehand.

One of my most memorable November hunt balls was the one themed *Red*, where I treated my friends to the rare sight of me in a dress! And not just any dress, a red taffeta strapless number, accessorized with a pair of full length red satin gloves. Jamie laughed when he saw me. I told him that I felt like my daughter Montana, playing dress-up as a young girl. He confirmed that's exactly what I looked like. Everyone puts great effort into their costumes; I guess they want to pay tribute to the months of hard work Louise puts into creating the stunning settings. There are no cheap, fun costumes, other than what I usually wear (though these still require considerable effort to put together). The Italians dress to look beautiful, tasteful, and luxurious, *la bella figura* at play. The surroundings are always matched to the theme, to provide the backdrop to the night of partying. For the *Red* hunt ball, red table linen, glasses, lights, candles and chili peppers helped create the dramatic scenery for the dinner and dancing.

Another year, the *Bollywood* theme saw Louise festoon the venue with lavish swathes of rich colored sari material - pinks, greens and reds. Dramatic Indian statues watched over proceedings and the air was heavy with incense. I remember the 80 year-old Count from the neighboring estate looking particularly magnificent dressed as a maharaja. No one had recognized me in my long, black wig and jeweled Indian pajamas, my eyes thick with Kohl. Louise, registering it was indeed me - put me in a funk with her comment,

Nita, you look like a transvestita!

Seeing the other *Bollywood* stars did not help my mood - a parade of skinny, sexy, sari-wearing and midriff-baring womanly women! So when I got the invitation for the next ball, a celebration of Louise's 40th birthday, themed *1001 Arabian Nights*, I was determined to figure out something more Nita-friendly, because there was no way I was coming as a belly dancer, the most obvious costume of choice.

A few weeks before my scheduled arrival into Florence, I e-mailed Louise to ask if she could please arrange a ride for me from Florence to Il Borro. She wrote back saying that probably Fabiola and Christian would have room for me. I replied my thanks and mentioned that I'd also need space for my snake. Louise responded quickly,

Nita! What on earth are you doing?

At a loss for another option, I told her I was coming as a snake charmer,

Don't give me a hard time; you have no idea how difficult it was to book an airplane ticket for a snake who is demanding a first-class seat!

Finding my snooty companion was no small feat, even in LA, land of make- believe and props. After visits to *Toys R Us* and numerous magic shops, and sending my *Desperately*

Seeking Snake outreach e-mail, I finally found my hissing friend at a toy store in town.

The weekend arrived for the *1001 Arabian Nights* event. The village of Il Borro was predominantly filled with party guests but, as is frequently the case, there were other non-party people staying there too. The evening of the ball, I was crossing the medieval bridge on my way to the main villa. Having their photos taken at this picturesque spot, a glorious sunset behind them, were the most lovely, elegant bride and groom. The tableau was magnificent, tasteful, so classically Italian - except the scene is then paused. The camera pans away and the eyes of the bridal party follow those of the photographer to alight on *someone,* possibly a woman, clad in a gigantic black and gold brocade and feather turban and black silk pajamas, carrying a flute and with what would appear to be a bright red and yellow, seven-foot, stuffed snake wrapped around her neck!

At each year's event, after we've admired each others' costumes at the early evening cocktail party, we leave the children and head to the *Sala di Caccia* for a lavish dinner before moving on to the ballroom to dance until the small hours. Then, the evening far from over, we go back to the main villa to sit around as a guest or two plays the grand piano; someone else usually picks up a guitar to give us a few more tunes. We sing; have pillow fights; discuss love, war, child-rearing, business, marriage and extra-marital affairs - no one believes I've never had one!

And then, around 5.00am I find myself, high heels in hand, walking along a wooded path, back to my room. It is freezing cold but I hardly notice the temperature or the rips in my stockings from the dancing. I'm thinking that here I am, at a party with a predominantly mid 30s crowd, out of my league in age, wealth and beauty. I look up at the moon,

And I actually think I'm one of them!

I laugh my ass off!

The delights of the weekend are still not over. The next morning, Sunday, and a few hardy souls, usually just me, head out for a bit more hunting with Jamie and his dog on the Il Borro estate. I adore Jamie; his values, authenticity and kindness, not to mention that he's drop-dead gorgeous. No matter if I'd only had three hours sleep, I'd never miss an opportunity to be with him, outdoors, and in one of the most beautiful settings in Tuscany. Jamie works incredibly hard and travels extensively and any spare minute he has, he wants to be with Louise and the kids, so I take advantage of any time I can have with him at Il Borro.

After a few hours of scoreless hunting (always the case when I accompany anyone), we go back to the villa. This is more of a family time with the kids running in and out and the parents lounging around, everyone talking over the night before and catching up with friends, some of whom they may not see again until next year's party. There is, of course, more food. We enjoy a Sunday afternoon spread of pasta, ribs, *bistecca fiorentina*, wine, breads and chocolate pastries. It's all very relaxed, very informal.

Most of us go our own way by 5.00pm on Sunday, certain that we'll be seeing each other the next year, because we always do. It really is a fairytale of a weekend and I count my many blessings as I head back to Florence and *The Florentine* to see what the week will bring…already wondering what next year's hunt ball theme will be.

Extra! Extra!

I'd never worked on a newspaper before *The Florentine*, not on a high school magazine, a college paper nor a community newsletter. In fact, I'd never even been a regular newspaper reader. As a child, I first became riveted to the news after seeing JFK assassinated on TV and since then my preferred mode of keeping up with the events of the day and the world is either by watching CNN, whether at home or in hotel rooms, or by listening to the radio. I keep any reading time for books. So what I actually knew about the newspaper business as we ventured into the brave new world of *The Florentine* was, well, limited.

I was comforted that our first managing editor *did* seem to know the business and trusted that she knew the rules and conventions for putting out a credible newspaper. After a few editions though, as I looked over the front pages, I was shocked to realize just how boring the headlines were. Examples from the first issue included: *Architect Isozaki revises Uffizi plans*; *Traffic Restrictions End in Florence*; *Historic City Centre Shops Risk Closure*. Not one of them made me curious or intrigued to read further.

Then the fun started. Initially with Tony, and later with Linda, a future managing editor, I'd go through the articles to be included in the paper and work on titles for each of them. I was most concerned about the front page headlines. The game is to compel people to pick up the paper, to attract readers. After several months of these weekly

123

brainstorming sessions, we learned a few tricks of the trade and at last the attention-grabbers started to pop up in our heads more quickly.

The easiest headlines to come up with were those using alliteration. If you dip into any issue after the first few, you'll see some of these starting to make it to the news pages. Some examples include: *Taken to Tax for Toxicity,* a story about city officials being in trouble for failing to take action against airborne pollution; *Botero Bronzes Burgled,* the report of the theft of some Fernando Botero statues from a foundry in Pietrasanta and; *Clooney Stays Cozy In Como,* an article playing down the rumors that *Gorgeous George* was planning to sell his villa in Laglio, a small fishing town near Lake Como.

Another headline-creating technique was making a play on words. Our attempts at these would often have us in stitches. A favorite example of this style was: *Pasta in Hot Water* which told of an investigation by Italy's anti-trust authority into whether or not price hikes by pasta makers genuinely reflected the rising cost of raw materials or were the result of collaborative price-fixing by greedy manufacturers. Another, *Weighty Issues Cramp Style* told of accusations that the fashion industry only paid lip-service to the promotion of positive body image for women of all sizes given that skinny, undernourished teenage waifs continued to be its models of choice. *Italy's Biggest Draw* reported on the *Cezanne a Firenze* event which saw the largest attendance ever at an art exhibition in Italy.

Another way to trigger snappy one-liners involved using a well known phrase or saying. *Shaken Not Stirred* covered the Tuscan location of some opening scenes from a James Bond film; *Putting the Squeeze on the Squeegee* told of the crackdown on unsolicited car windshield washing and; *Camorra does Dirty Laundry* headlined an investigation into mafia money laundering in luxury hotels. The challenge was not to be *too* obvious - we didn't always succeed!

Often, the well-known phrase we'd use for a headline was from a movie or song title. We churned out a lot of these: *One Flew Over the Cupola* shared the story of peregrine falcons nesting in Il Duomo; *Three Coins in A Bloodbath* told of a political activist putting red dye in Rome's Trevi Fountain; and *Pitti in Pink* reported on the possibility of women's clothing being introduced at *Pitti Uomo*, Florence's traditionally male fashion week.

Coming up with ideas always worked better when there were two of us on the job, bouncing around all sorts of suggestions, often last minute or late at night when we were tired and a bit slap happy, just wanting to get an issue finished. I remember Tony and me in tears from laughter during one late night session when we came up with: *Bimbo Breaches the Fort!* The children's clothing market is called *Pitti Bimbo* and Fortezza da Basso was the venue where it was setting up.

After a year, we had a collection of favorites that we'd just randomly shout out for a laugh because we'd used them so much: *face-lift, launches, makes an entrance,* and *make-over* probably rank the highest as most-used expressions. We applied them ad infinitum to people, buildings, art-works, government plans, cultural events and much more.

It was a surprise to me, to learn that so much brainpower was involved in coming up with so few words, but creating headlines was a new-found skill for which I discovered I had a knack,

Old Dog Learns New Tricks.

The Sting

Besides covering the news and events, we wanted to develop some recurring columns for *The Florentine*. From the beginning, I was eager to hunt down the big interviews with famous and, if possible, *in*famous people: chefs, artists, fashion designers, politicians and the Florentine nobility included. I also wanted to do interviews with *everyday* people like the man who sings folk songs on the Ponte Vecchio at night, one of the *carabinieri* (police), a barista and an English teacher. Basically, I was interested in everyone. I needed a writer to be in charge of this column; to find the right people, set up the interviews (and let me do the glamorous ones!) and then write them up for inclusion in *The Florentine*. My first idea was to do something like the interviews on the last page of *Vanity Fair*, a set of 20 or so standard questions. I put together a draft of my ideas and went to my *go-to-gal*, Suzi Jenkins, asking if she would be interested in managing the column.

Suzi's first response was: *yes*. Only then did she ask me exactly what would be involved. I said I wanted to get interviews with people such as the mayor; the director of the Uffizi Museum; Wanda Ferragamo; Bona Frescobaldi (the matriarch of the wine family); the American ambassador. And then I confided,

…but to be honest Suzi, the real point of doing all this, interesting though all these people are, is so I can get an interview with Sting.

Now, if you're an Ally McBeal fan, think of the storyline where the lawyer brings a case against Sting on behalf of a husband, accusing Sting of *making his wife fall in love with him when he sang.* Let's just say they could have cast me as the wife in question with very little direction. To this day many people believe that the fact Sting has an estate in Tuscany was actually *the* reason I chose Florence as a place to live.

Anyhow, my revelation to Suzi was met with a curious response from my normally can-do, fun, sarcastic, irreverent and never-at-a-loss-for-words friend: *silence* - and a distinctly awkward silence at that,

Suzi, are you still there? She spoke at last, her tone far from thrilled,

Oh, so that's why you're asking me to do this column.

I was clearly missing something and had no choice but to ask her what it might be. Suzi asked if I was *really* unaware that her ex-partner (and father of her son) was the manager of Sting's Tuscan estate. I swore to her I'd had no idea! She'd thought I was angling for her to use her contact to get the interview, something she'd never do. Fortunately she believed what was, after all, my genuine surprise on learning of her connection.

Two weeks later, we received our first request for a subscription to *The Florentine.* I looked at the signature: Gordon Sumner! Sting was the newspaper's first subscriber.

I have had many near misses in my quest to meet my soul-mate. He would be sighted at a store in town while I was at lunch two blocks away, or he'd arrive at an art exhibition opening 20 minutes after I left. I attended a concert he gave in Florence, and my girlfriend saw me leaning so far over the banister, she was afraid I would jump into his lap. Walking home from the event, my head filled with his beautiful music, I was talking with Montana who had called me from LA. I told her that it was weird being so close to him. I confided in her,

Montana, of all the things I have wanted to do in my life, or have had the goals to do, Sting is the last holdout. What will happen, if and when, I finally do meet him? It's kind of like I'll have nothing to live for.

Montana's response,

You know Mom, I find that sad.

Sad but true.

I heard the next day that there was a dinner with Sting, to which another friend would have gotten me invited - if only she'd known of my obsession!

I never did get to interview the great man while I was working on *The Florentine*, but there's still time...

Very recently I returned from an overseas trip and checked my e-mail and found an instruction from Louise Ferragamo to *get over to Florence*. In two days time, Sting was going to make an appearance at their family owned estate, Il Borro. Trust me, for a few minutes I seriously considered hopping on the next flight.

A couple of days later she e-mailed again and told me Sting, for whatever reason, had been a no-show. I guess he heard I couldn't make it.

Take Me Out to the Ball Game

I remember one time, as a young girl, driving home with my mother, when she turned on the radio to hear the result of the baseball game. I was shocked,

Why do you care about the score?

My mother, like me had no interest in sports whatsoever. Her answer, however, made sense,

I want to know what kind of mood your dad will be in when he comes home, and whether I need to bother to cook a nice dinner or not.

Over the years my father had season tickets to the *Detroit Lions, Tigers, Pistons* and *Redwings* - for the uninitiated that covers football of the American kind, baseball, basketball and hockey. He'd take my equally sports obsessed brothers to see the games so I wasn't even required to feign some kind of interest. And, fortunately he was happy to take me to the movies, Broadway musicals and shopping. My lack of enthusiasm for sports continued for years. And then I met Tony.

At the time, Tony, as well as being a typical red-blooded, sports-loving American male, also happened to be the financial vice-president of the *Seattle Supersonics*, a NBA basketball team. It didn't take long for me to be taken in by the glitz surrounding the games and the glamour of the front row seats. Several friends accused me of marrying Tony for his *Sonic* tickets, which I've never actually denied. At the time basketball was to Seattle what Hollywood is to LA (the Sonics have since moved to Oklahoma). The buzz around the *Sonics* was huge, especially given they'd won the championship the year before. I became totally absorbed in the excitement of it all: the end-to-end pace of the game; the skill and lightning reactions of the players; the team selection and dynamic; and, yes, finding out how much the players earned and looking out for what their wives wore to the games.

As to the rules and plays of the game, Tony was very generous with me, answering my most idiotic questions. Finding a thirsty student, he enjoyed explaining the finer nuances that determined a team's success. I learned to watch how the players played *away from the ball*; I began to appreciate how much the game was about defense rather than just scoring points; I formed my own opinions about what was working and what wasn't. One night, cocky in my new knowledge, and having dinner after the game with Lenny Wilkins, the Sonics' coach, and his wife, I found myself critiquing Lenny on his substitutions. Before I could make a further ass of myself, Tony reminded me that although I was infinitely knowledgeable about the game, Lenny had just been honored as one of the *winningest* coaches in the NBA.

This new-found love of basketball spilled over into watching other sports, live and on TV, including football, tennis and golf. Tony describes me as the perfect wife on the basis of this alone, marveling that I'll watch sports *even when he's not there*. For further evidence of my conversion, let's just say that my two children, Jordan and Montana are not named after geographical locations…

I didn't have to be in Italy long to know that for Italians the *beautiful game* is *calcio*, known as soccer in the US, and as football - of the *kick-it-don't-pick-it-up* variety - to most of the rest of the world. *Fiorentina* is the name of Florence's soccer team and like in other Italian cities, the loyalty and passion to the club makes US fans look amateurish and neglectful in their sporting allegiance. In contrast, one of the things that surprised me in my early days in Italy was that I didn't find anywhere near the level of patriotic spirit and national pride I'd expected. I learned that this was, in large part, due to the fact that Italy had only been a united country for a little over 100 years. A legacy of this is that Italians identify much more with their city-state than with the nation as a whole. One consequence of this more local connection is the fierce support for their soccer teams such as *AC Milan, Roma, Lazio* and of course *Fiorentina*. Italians do manage a potent display of unity for the duration of the World Cup; although I can even think of exceptions to that. I remember Leo, one of my *Florentine* partners refusing to watch Italy in one of the qualifying games on the basis that he couldn't stand seeing the *Juventus* (a Turin team) players do well.

Early on in Florence, when I heard of an occasion that managed to combine my love of watching sport with another great passion, that of tradition and ritual, my attention was caught. Dating back to at least the 15th century, in many cities and towns, there is an annual event that pits the historical districts against each other in a sporting tradition of some kind. Most famous, there's the *Palio* horse race in Siena and the *Giostra del Saracino,* a joust, in Arezzo. In Florence, June 24th each year sees the *Calcio Storico,* basically, traditional football in costumes.

Said to be originally played by aristocratic nobles in celebration of the feast of St. John, Florence's patron saint, today's participants in *Calcio Storico* wear different colors to show their allegiance to particular quarters of the city: blue for Santa Croce, red for Santa Maria Novella; white for Santo Spirito and; green for San Giovanni. A parade precedes the main event, everyone wearing richly decorated costumes. Solemn music accompanies the procession to the Piazza Santa Croce, which has been transformed into a stadium; it's met with a fanfare of trumpets and a wildly cheering crowd. One year, Tony managed to track down some not inexpensive tickets, so we could see the action first hand.

As I watched the players warming up, I was intrigued. Florence is a *small town* and I had never before seen such burly men walking around the streets. Where did these thugs come from with their shaved heads and shirtless tattooed bodies, flexing their muscles with great menace? And why were they warming up by shadow boxing, throwing punches into the air rather than running on the spot or stretching their limbs? They certainly had nothing in common with the well-groomed Italian league stars, so often accused of being more concerned with the perfection of their hair than their performance on the field.

While perhaps lacking the finesse of *Serie A* and the skill and glamour provided by the likes of Beckham and Ronaldo, we were still expecting a soccer game of sorts, just with some kind of ancient twist. It turned out to be more primitive than historical. What we didn't expect, of all things, was a spectacle within which Russell Crowe, clad for gladiatorial combat, would have seemed quite at home. We were stunned! It was hard to believe Florence, birthplace of the European Renaissance, known for the beauty and refinement of its traditions and art, a place in which butchers recite Dante and taxi-drivers hum Tosca, was host to this barbaric event.

The 54 players, which made up the two teams, were *fist fighting* five seconds after the referee, dressed in a doublet and knickerbockers and an ostrich-feathered velvet cap, brandished his sword to signal the start of the event. Within a few minutes, stretcher bearers appeared, running on and off, Keystone cop-like, to deal with the injured. A number of additional referees, all in traditional dress, took their own lives into their hands by showering the marauding combatants with water, as if trying to separate pit-bulls at an illegal dog fight. Tony and I could hardly believe what we were watching: bruising, blood and breakages.

My born-again status as a sports spectator had trained me to follow the ball. The violence, as far as I could see, had no obvious connection with gaining possession and driving the ball to its target. Goal-scoring was, I'd been assured, still the aim of the game, achieved by throwing the red and white ball over a wooden wall found at each end of the playing area. The manic cheering around me, however, was a response to the fighting rather than the scoring of points. The winner of this first match of brawl and destruction would then play against the winner of a similar game between the teams representing the other two historic quarters of the city. If, after the weekend of combat, anyone survived, the last souls standing had the honor of being named champions for the year and given *a pile of steaks of a weight equivalent to that of a white calf.*

For some relief from the on-pitch battle, I turned my attention to the spectators. Again, just as with the players warming up, I didn't seem to recognize these people, full of blood lust and braying for more brutality. When, the next day, I asked my Italian teacher who the participants were - both players and spectators - Catia, a native Florentine who had never attended the display herself, wasn't sure. She suggested that they might be factory workers or car mechanics, maybe security guards?

A *Florentine* article covered the *Calcio Storico*, which included the suggestion that the event, and its counterparts in other towns and cities, served to channel the *normal aggressions* of the community and contributed to the relatively low rate of violent crime in Italy. It was a nice idea. The *Calcio Storico* was in fact stopped for some years; there's a debate over whether this was because it was genuinely deemed to be too violent, or whether this was given as an excuse not to have to come up with the considerable funding that putting on the event requires. Either way, this Greco-Roman *wrestling-come-boxing-come-rugby-come-free-for-all* is very much alive today.

My personal distaste for the event is hardly likely to bear influence on the future of *Calcio Storico*. Apparently even the armies of Charles V, storming into Florence, cannons firing, to restore the Medici government, hadn't been enough to interrupt the young nobles in the middle of their game. Still, I'm strangely glad I went…even though once was more than enough!

You've Got a Friend in Me

After a visit to the café and market, nothing else was ever typical about my day working on *The Florentine*. If it was a day we went to print, then I'd definitely head to the office and work on the last of the editing, proof-reading and finalizing the headlines. I'd also help with the English translations for the advertisements of our Italian clients. Another reason to go into the office was for scheduled meetings, whether with a potential new writer or advertiser, or maybe to orient a student intern or interview someone for an article.

Most of my work, however, was done outside the office. If I was writing, then I worked better alone in my apartment, but more often than not I'd be found out and about meeting people, visiting new places, attending events and going after advertisers. One day I could be at a meeting with the *Comune*, the city council; the next, I might be visiting a university or museum director. Maybe the day after, I'd enjoy un caffè with a designer, a teacher, a politician or a gallery owner. The day after that might see me interviewing an antique restorer, a musician, a chef and even, on occasion, a poet.

As a person endlessly curious about people, I was in nirvana. In both my personal and professional life I've always been a compulsive interviewer. This is still a constant annoyance to my kids who are known to warn new friends who come to our house that they'll be *in for a grilling*. And at a party, if Tony wants to know more about someone, he'll instruct:

Nita, get his story!

Whereas many people are afraid of being considered intrusive, I have noticed that most people actually like it when another person shows interest in them. And that's what I am, interested in other people. I'm curious about what they do, why they do it, how they do it. Whether interviewing for *The Florentine*, or just meeting people at dinner, in a shop, or in the line for gas, the questions come easily,

Tell me what a day in your life looks like? What do you miss when you're away from Florence? What were the ideals or values that you learned from your parents? What do you want to pass on to your children? What are common misunderstandings that people have about Italians?

People's stories, from whatever walk of life they come, are just an infinite source of fascination to me. I have always loved the intimacy of conversation. And this was my job! Granted, it would have been even more dream-like if I got *paid* for doing this thing I loved so much. Still, the unique and special opportunities to discover and share others' stories during my time at *The Florentine*, and the contributions to the readers and the local community I was able to make as a result, were what made me happier and more fulfilled than in any other job in my life. Given that I've had the luxury, good judgment or maybe just luck, of never having had a job I didn't love, this is no small pronouncement.

From time to time, my partners at *The Florentine* accused me of *only* interviewing and writing about my friends. The reality was, it worked the other way around; the people I interviewed and wrote about *became* my friends. Somehow, as well as being driven by a streak of endless curiosity, I also have a way of getting people to open up, a gift that I treasure for the way it's allowed me to get close to people quickly and make a special connection on the basis of just one meeting. And when I met people I liked through work, who I may not have had a further business reason to see again, I had no hesitation in requesting we be friends.

One example of this occurred after I'd received an e-mail from Rafaella Antoniazzi, an executive with the luxurious Lungarno Hotels. She complimented us on the relatively new *Florentine* and asked to meet to discuss how we might have a copy in each of the hotels' rooms. Rafaella quickly impressed me; she was intelligent, sensitive, astute and widely traveled. Our conversation roamed seamlessly and openly from family, to politics, then to business. At the end of the meeting, as she was walking us to the lobby door, I said,

I really like you. Do you think we could be friends?

She had never received such a request,

That's so American!

But she was delighted and said yes, of course. Close friends we became and remain.

This integrated life worked well for me. My partners were my family and my clients and writers and interview subjects became my friends. My schedule of obligations and duties were my much enjoyed social life. Another way this integration of personal and professional life showed up, much more strongly than the delineation of these two things in the US, was in the way I never felt the need to *put on a professional hat*. For example, in Italy, the value placed on being a loving mother meant that talking about your children and the challenges of motherhood with business associates was completely acceptable and not a topic you would be expected to hold back from sharing. The very fact of *being a mother* was something that would immediately gain you credibility and respect. For me, this contributed to a sense of truly being myself at all times and not having to worry about not appearing 'professional'; it also meant that in greeting my close friends or on my meeting the *presidente* of the *Region* for just the second time, I would feel equally comfortable with the double cheek kiss!

A friend of mine once told me how she had gone about forming a community of friends when new to the intimidating metropolis of New York City. I followed her advice when I moved to Santa Fe from Seattle and then to Florence. Every Friday night, I invited people whom I had met that week and thought were nice or interesting, over to my apartment for dinner. Everyone likes invitations, even from people whom they don't know well. This proved true with the Florentines too, who have lived in their city for their entire lives and already have an existing close circle of friends and family with whom they regularly spend time. People always accepted my invites. However, I learned not to expect immediate reciprocal invitations, at least not until after several further invitations from me. I found that I almost had to intrude to insinuate myself into their seemingly impenetrable patterns of friendship. This was not because I wasn't liked or wanted, or they hadn't enjoyed the occasions they'd attended at my invitation, but because they simply weren't used to thinking of me, given their own established social circles.

I realized I had finally *made it*, when I came back to Florence for my third year on September 1st after spending the summer in LA. My cell phone started ringing immediately. I was in! All Italians leave Florence for the month of August, and everything shuts down; it's hard to find a food, clothing or hardware store open and it's the few storekeepers that *do stay open*, who have to put signs on their doors to announce this very fact. The custom is, that when you come back into the city after *ferie,* you call all your friends to see how they are doing and to make plans for un caffè. Here I was afraid of having to start over again after being away for three months, but nothing of the sort - I was on the list, in the circle.

Looking back on my time in Florence I realize that many of my female friendships came about not just because I was able to meet so many great women through my work, or even that I was brave enough to reach out and ask to be friends or make them a dinner invitation. Rather, it was these things combined with the fact that I was a very different kind of girlfriend than my Italian friends were used to having. Without exception, they preferred the quality of our friendship to the usual Italian kind.

More than one Italian woman shared with me that a deep-seated competitiveness seems to exist between Italian women. This frequently got in the way of their making close female friendships of the intimate, secrets shared and hopes and worries-confided-in kind. This competitiveness is all-encompassing, obvious and ugly. It's typified by the critical *once-over* an Italian woman will give every other woman who walks into the room, checking out how she is dressed, how thin she is (or not), the size of her boobs, the length of her hair.

An American friend who is married to an Italian man told me that, at the beach in August, she's appalled at the way the Italian women so frequently discuss who is thinnest amongst them, judging every passing woman in a similar fashion. Another friend told me that she simply doesn't trust her female friends. She knows that they are not looking out for her happiness and in fact, are doing quite the opposite. Her 'friends' talk poorly about her behind her back, would envy her every success (career, men, appearance) and actually be gleeful about her perceived failures. I found this sad, given the love, support and fun my own close female friends have given me in life, and equally, the fulfillment I get from being there for them in good times and bad.

In Florence, with new friends, I refused to join in conversations I'd see as either judging someone based on factors of no relevance or, that were just out-and- out back-stabbing sessions. It is in my nature to be encouraging and supporting to others and as a result I developed close friendships with Italian women who found our relationship unique in that they didn't enjoy anything similar with other girlfriends.

I'm proud that a legacy of my time in Florence is that many Italian women formed *Nita-type* friendships amongst themselves, after meeting each other at my house *and* with people they would not have normally gotten to know within their usually closed circles. These close and nurturing friendships have survived and thrived. My heart is warmed that these women, who gave me so much while I lived in Florence, are 'in good hands' and being loved and nurtured by each other.

Mona Lisa's Dimples

Princess Natalia Guicciardini Strozzi is a real life princess. I met her at a party at the home of designer Roberto Cavalli. Natalia descends from the coming together through marriage of the Guicciardini counts and the Strozzi nobles, her father being Prince Guicciardini Strozzi. One of her Guicciardini ancestors was a famous historian and politician who employed none other than Niccolo Machiavelli as his secretary. The other branch of the family, the Strozzis, was made up of bankers who spent much of the Renaissance kept in exile by the Medicis, with whom they were locked in a continuous power struggle. Natalia's mother, Irina Reine, was born in Paris and her Russian and Polish background comes with its own fair share of distinguished heritage, one of her ancestors is *Saint* Stanislao Kostka no less.

Such family connections fascinate me, but the allure attached to Princess Natalia is not just of the very long ago kind. Sir Winston Churchill resides somewhere on her family tree. Her godfather was Gregory Peck. When she was four years old, and already obsessed with dance, Rudolf Nureyev, a family friend, staying at their house, *discovered her*, and by the time she was 14 years old, she was dancing with him at the Kirov Ballet. If all that wasn't glamorous enough, in a news item covered by *The Florentine*, an Italian genealogist made the claim, since confirmed, that Natalia Strozzi is a descendent of Lisa Gheradini del Giacondo, the woman who is said to have posed for Leonardo's *Mona Lisa*.

I found Natalia adorable - lively, sweet, friendly and warm. Yes, she did have a certain smile, though more of the open, enthusiastic, dimpled Shirley Temple kind than anything as enigmatic as that of the *Mona Lisa*. She told me she had written a book about her life, all 28 years of it: *Facile de Ricordare - Easy to Remember*. It was partly autobiographical and partly drew upon her rich ancestry. She had yet to have it translated into English, so we talked a little about the possibility of doing this through *The Florentine Press*, the publishing arm we'd developed alongside the newspaper.

Natalia had recently become involved with acting. She'd been working in Italy, but wanted to give Hollywood a try. I naturally wanted to help if I could. Two friends of mine from LA, Patti Detroit and Ronni Chasen (Ronni since tragically murdered in Beverly Hills), both very important in the film industry, were vacationing in Florence, so I brought them to meet Natalia. I also invited along my friend Nora Dempsey, the US Consul General. Part of her job was to meet visiting, influential Americans. I knew Nora, who like me, is originally from Detroit, would be interested to meet both my LA friends and the Strozzis and that they'd be similarly pleased to meet her.

Natalia asked us to meet her at Cuzona, her family's majestic country estate. Along with several palazzos in Florence, this estate has been part of the Strozzi family's holdings since the 16th Century. The magnificent tower of the impressive palazzo dates back to 1100. The estate includes acres of vineyards.

Irina was a regal and perfect hostess. Even in this relaxed country setting, she exuded grace, beauty and dignity. As we drank tea she entertained us with stories including how she first became aware of the man who would become her husband while they were both studying in Switzerland. They had apartments adjacent to each other, but for a long time never met although messages were exchanged via the landlord. It was months before they met face to face, and it wasn't until he had gone back to Italy, that he finally asked her on a date. The Prince came out to greet us. Elegant and formal in his conservative dark pinstripe suit, he stood by his wife and daughter, his presence commanding even as he drank his tea; he was clearly holding court.

During our tour of their palazzo, Natalia pointed out to us the paintings in the dining room, all portraits of the Medici,

We get pleasure that they (the Medici) who are all gone, have to eternally gaze upon us - still alive, well and eating plentifully. It's the ultimate triumph!

As we wandered through the gardens, Irina educated us about which grapes were used for either the red or white wines produced in the family business. We entered the caves of the centuries-old cantina, passing by the very first *Fiat* ever made - a tractor. In the cellars, it was humbling to look at the ancient wooden kegs, not confined to a museum, but still used to hold the aging wine. And everywhere, the family crest, carved into wooden beams, frescoed on the walls, or adorning the labels of the wine bottles that were either archived or displayed in the tasting room.

We hear a little too, of Tony Blair, the then English Prime Minister, who stayed at the palazzo for his summer visits in Tuscany. We learn of his hushed conversations to a President Clinton, admonishing him to *admit the truth* about a young intern named Monica; political intrigues, of course, nothing new in the Guicciardini-Strozzi history.

The visit over, we drove away down the tree-canopied road; the fairytale castle and the fairytale princess fading away. We all looked at each other, wondering if we had just awakened from the same dream: *did that just happen?* Nora laughed,

Look at us Nita! Who'd have thought that a couple of girls from Detroit would end up here?

Parenting in Paradise

Boating in the Galapagos, bungee jumping in Costa Rica, *too many churches Mom* in Spain, animal parks in Kenya; my kids got to travel a lot in their younger years. Having a severe case of the travel bug myself, I was committed that they have the worldly experiences and exposure to different cultures and languages that I'd not had in my own childhood and for which I'd much envied my peers. I knew that the best of my own life education came from my traveling days and I wanted my kids to get an early start on all that learning. We enjoyed many great family trips. But, while I was quite aware that living in Europe was my personal dream, part of that dream was about giving my kids the experience of living outside of the US and particularly to do this in the cultural wonder that is Europe.

By the time we actually made it happen, Jordan, my eldest, was in college and so wasn't going to be joining us, but Montana was 15 and going into ninth grade. She wasn't the happiest about leaving her friends in Santa Fe. We arrived in Florence a week before school started and she spent those first days not wanting to do anything. Even a gelato wouldn't entice her to leave the house with us to go to the Pitti Palace, the Uffizi or even for an evening stroll along the Arno. She did nothing. We didn't even have a working TV, so she just stayed around the house, pouted and read.

If Montana had been younger, I would have wanted to put her into an Italian school, but not being able to speak the language and about to start high school, I thought it would be too much for her to take on, so I enrolled her in the International School of Florence, where they taught in English. I was relieved when, from the first day of school, she made friends and was soon having fun. More than half her class was new, so no cliques had formed yet and she was able to join in easily. I was happy because she was happy. All was great...until we got report cards. Montana was not doing well.

I'd sum up my reaction by saying I opted for being angry over being empathetic to her situation. My deep attachment to her grades resulted in much drama, lost sleep (on my part), along with unsuccessful attempts to incentivize, manipulate, reward and punish. I met with her teachers and hired tutors for her, all to no avail in terms of her grades improving and much to the detriment of our relationship. Looking back, I definitely would have done some things differently. That we happened to be in Italy made it so much worse for me. There I was with all my dreams about giving my daughter this extraordinary opportunity and my long held visions of what it would be like for me and her to be together in such a wonderful place. None of my expectations were fulfilled.

During our first year in Florence, Tony and I would go on day trips every Sunday to the small towns in and around Tuscany. Montana never wanted to go with us, or we would have to bribe her to make her go. We also wanted to take the fullest advantage of being not just in Italy, but in Europe, hoping to introduce our daughter to Paris, Amsterdam and Vienna. Again, she wasn't interested. We didn't want to leave her alone, so we didn't go ourselves. What Montana *did* want to do, was chill with her friends. Like any teenager, I guess.

In addition to her poor grades, the International School was expensive and I thought Montana wasn't getting enough of an authentic Italian experience. So after the first year, I enrolled her in an Italian school. This was a mistake, a disaster in fact. She was not happy. We argued: about school; about where she was, or rather where she said she was; about whether she was smoking; about her lack of exercise; about opportunities she wasn't taking; in the end, just about everything.

For those who are looking to spend a year in Italy or moving there longer term, the schooling of your kids will require some tough decisions. You'll have to take into account the age of your children, how long you'll be in Italy, and most importantly, their personalities. I think if they are younger, I would put them into an Italian school, to give them a real chance to integrate and experience something different, but that may not work for all kids.

Someone asked me during this first year in Florence whether I was happy. I guess I've always experienced, and therefore come to expect, that happiness is fleeting, no matter where you are. In giving my answer, I explained that in Florence the highs were higher and the lows were much, much lower, especially since I didn't have my girlfriends to consult and talk things through.

Montana's performance at school and her behavior generally, along with my inability to deal effectively with it, was certainly giving me my worse low ever. I also realized there was something different about it: I was cutting myself off, hiding from people, a thing I never do, and over-reacting to things in general. I went to the doctor to see if maybe I needed anti-depressants. I wanted to feel more able to cope with it all and to be there for my daughter. The doctor gave me, what, surprisingly came as good news,

Nita, you're experiencing the first signs of the menopause!

Before trying hormone replacement she wanted to prescribe me minerals. She did - they worked!

Back to feeling sane again, I was able to see that while I would still have been getting upset by the same things, the onset of menopause was blowing my responses out of proportion. What's more, this overreaction was actually making things worse. I realized that most of my friends had also had trying times with their teenagers and most, like me, felt that they'd made some mistakes and wished they'd done some things differently. I'm not saying I shouldn't have reacted at all, or not tried to set boundaries, but I could have done both in a much more controlled and effective way.

When Italian school didn't work out, we tried home-schooling. Not a success. It was then that Montana made the decision to go back to the US to live with Tony in LA, where he'd set up his new business. I was devastated. Beyond painful, it felt as if my heart was being wrenched out of my body.

Those around me, even if they didn't ask outright, were clearly thinking,

Your husband is in LA, your daughter wants to go back, isn't it time for you to go back, too? If your family is supposedly what is most important to you, why would you stay here, when they need you there?

I had to do some major soul-searching. If I focused solely on what would help Montana most, I recognized that what she desperately needed was to have some time and space away from me. I imagine that having me as a mother, with all the love, encouragement and help I give, can be totally amazing - and also totally overwhelming in not such a good way!

In showing enthusiasm and support for anything in which Montana showed even the mildest interest (as I wish I'd experienced from my own parents), I realized I'd overdone things. If Montana mentioned she liked singing, I would find the best voice teacher in Santa Fe and have her in lessons the next week. If she had trouble with math, she had a private tutor. I went way beyond encouragement, not being able to tolerate the thought of her interests not being fully supported, or that she had to struggle in any way. I only wanted my daughter to have what she needed to feel loved and have a successful and fulfilling life. But I realized the result of my very best intentions was that I was stunting Montana's own ability to work things through, to make her own choices and take responsibility for them - to show self-determination. She needed to discover *herself* and clearly differentiate herself from me - and to do that she needed be away from my immediate influence.

Before she left, I said to her,

Montana, I just want you to know that if you want me to be back with you in LA, I will leave here immediately. Nothing, not the paper, not my life in Florence, nor my friends here, would cause me to hesitate, even for a minute.

Her response:

Mom, I know that. It's other people that don't understand that you and I need this. I know they think you're selfish, but you and I know this is the right thing for me.

Even with this assurance, I still questioned myself. I have very, very few regrets in my life, but if I could do one thing over, I would have kept Montana at the International School. Although I was not impressed with the quality of the education offered there, or with the lack of support she was given academically, she was happy and would have probably stayed with me in Italy had I kept her enrolled there.

The whole experience was a tough time for our relationship, but thankfully our strong love for each other is of the unconditional kind. Living in Florence was my dream, not hers, and we both moved on from this in ways that worked for each of us, me staying in Florence and her picking up again in the US. It wasn't to be the end of testing times for us, but throughout we have continued to have a close and loving bond.

At my recent birthday, Tony, Jordan and Montana each gave me a *Top Ten List* of their memorable moments with me. Two of Montana's items related to Italy. The first one of these:

Even though I hated you for it at the time, when you moved me to Italy, I really found out who I was and what I was capable of and it made me who I am today.

In the second she wrote,

Accepting the fact that I needed to leave Italy and move to California, to live with Dad, so that you and I could come to have a relationship again.

I've written a lot of books about relationships and people have asked me several times to write a book specifically on parenting; I laugh out loud at the suggestion. My kids are wonderful and fortunately I have great connections with both of them, but in the area of parenting I feel neither wise nor successful. I do feel grateful that I have these incredible people in my life, but I take no credit for their awesomeness.

A Pristine Sistine Visit

Yes, you can actually arrange a private visit to the Sistine Chapel. And if you do, you can stand alone, as I did, far enough away from the altar to take in the whole wall behind it. And so you are able, not just to witness the legendary ceiling, but to truly experience the power of Michelangelo's masterpiece: *The Last Judgment*. The novelty of this, of course, assumes your ideal view of the second coming of Christ and the apocalypse comes unimpeded by other people, loaded with backpacks the size of small houses and waving guidebooks open to photographs of the very same work of art that, if they were just to lower their book a little, they, and you, could all see for real.

You don't have to be a Head of State, a member of a royal family, or George Clooney to enjoy this potentially life-changing experience. It can still be yours, albeit you will require €1800 and an advance booking to secure it. You can, if you want, bring your personal entourage; if you don't have one of these and you'd like some help to defray the cost, consider inviting up to 29 of your family and friends to share the experience, or even, to enter into a spirit of forgiveness, one or two people you don't like very much. Imagine: no wait; no lines; no pushing, shoving and bumping; no one else to spoil the precious sanctity of this awe-inspiring sight.

Of course for you, or your small select posse to get *in*, the masses first have to get *out*, so you'll need to wait until 5.00pm to gain access. My suggestion as to what to do beforehand, to take full advantage of your trip to the Vatican, is to visit the Christian necropolis of Scavi which was excavated below Vatican City in the 1940s. The archaeological diggings were funded by Pope Piux XI, who wished to be buried as close to the apostle Peter as possible. It is alleged that the much revered St. Peter is buried here because of the closeness of the site to the Circus of Nero, where he is said to have been martyred.

You must book the Scavi tour weeks in advance, requesting your language of choice. Your guide will be a novitiate priest. Speaking to friends who have also visited, the tour seems to vary according to which priest you get, ranging from a mystery and suspense-filled *Da Vinci Code*-type exploration of the authenticity of St. Peter's bones (which was the one I attended), to a merely very interesting experience. You are guided, for an hour and a half, through an excavated street between well-preserved tombs and mausoleums and an ancient graveyard, before eventually returning to the Basilica.

The tour is limited to groups of 10-15. While this restriction is to assist with the conservation of the site, it has the additional benefit of helping you prepare for the privacy and exclusivity of your soon-to-be-experienced Sistine Chapel encounter.

The hordes have now departed for an evening of the many other delights Rome has to offer, leaving you to the joy of a quick and easy passage through security and into the grand and quiet halls of the Vatican Museums. Of course the guards accompany you, but this only adds to the luxury of the experience; it appears that their only job is to serve as your personal valets, to open and close doors for you - well, to lock, unlock and secure them, at any rate.

Previous memories, and those shared by friends about their visits to the Vatican Museums, consist of rushing and maneuvering through the crowds in an apparent race to get to the star attraction of the Sistine Chapel. As a result, the many halls and galleries, filled with some of the world's most precious art, are missed; most visitors not even conscious they exist. Sculpture from ancient Rome, a room filled with the paintings of Raphael and the amazing hall of tapestries and maps, are just a few of the treasures that remain unexamined by the millions.

When you enter alone, however, something is very different; it's as if you are not in a museum at all, but rather a private villa or palazzo, no longer a tourist but an invited guest. At the same time as you are overwhelmed by the grandeur, there is a feeling of intimacy, the surroundings revealing their true selves to you alone.

Take your time; the main event is waiting for you, not going anywhere. Wander into the gardens, linger, and be moved by the same sculptures that perhaps inspired Michelangelo. Let the expectation build, there is no chance of disappointment or anti-climax. Then, as the sun begins to set, enter the Sistine Chapel.

Stop.

Breathe.

This is a moment you will remember for the rest of your life. And for now, the moment is all yours.

Reservations to visit the Scavi are only accepted in writing by e-mail: scavi@fsp.va by fax: (39-06) 6987-3017, or directly in the Excavations Office.

Enquiries about private after-hours tours of the Vatican Museums can be made at visitespeciali.musei@scv.va

Frantic for Ferragamo

My girlfriend Abra was visiting from LA. Her daughter, Rory Edelman, is a successful fashion designer with her own label *RoryBeca*. Abra had been 'commissioned' to buy textiles for her line while she was in Italy. I was very pleased to be able to introduce her to my new landlady! Independent of the Ferragamos, Louise Ferragamo's own business involves arranging for designers *outside* of Italy to have clothing and accessories produced *within* Italy. Her clients have included Ralph Lauren and many Danish designers. I asked her if she could take Abra to Prato, a town on the outskirts of Florence which is the center of the textile and clothing industry. Of course I wanted in on the action too. I would *go along for the ride.*

Louise knows every warehouse in Prato and was able to tell Abra which places were good for linens, which ones best for knits and so on. Not only did she know where every fabric could be found, going to these places with Louise opened much more than the front doors - each owner's face lit up when she walked in, they couldn't do enough for her and her 'clients'. At this time, I didn't know Louise that well; our interactions had been connected to the apartment, things such as getting the lease signed and the dishwasher fixed. Having adored her from our first meeting, I appreciated having this time to get to know her better. After a few hours of purchasing, we went for lunch and got down to getting better acquainted.

Being the chronic interviewer that I am, I grilled away,

How did you meet Jamie? What was it like to be part of such an important family? What is it like living on the family estate?

Louise shared a little about how she met her husband and her positive experience of becoming part of the Ferragamo family. When she met Jamie, the couple spent most of their time at her small apartment. She had little exposure to, or indeed any idea of, the grandeur in which his family lived. Also, her own upbringing and outlook meant that she never expected or hoped to be supported by a husband, or a husband's family. She was very comfortable taking care of herself. And so, the Ferragamos love Louise for her independence and the fact that she is clearly not looking to take advantage of their wealth and power, all of them respecting her for these lovely, decent qualities.

We went on to talk about our kids, her family in Denmark, why I had come to Italy, the coming together of the newspaper. After an hour, I adored her even more; she's kind, unimpressed with herself and openly appreciative of my direct and self-deprecating sense of humor. We became intimate immediately.

Confident that it would be clear by then I enjoyed Louise for her company and beautiful self, rather than her connections, I couldn't help *doing-a-Nita;*

So now that we're friends Louise, does this mean that I can get uno sconto at Ferragamo?

Her reaction was surprise, not at my *chutzpah*, but at the fact I wanted to shop at *Ferragamo*, thinking that the style may be a little too conservative for my taste. On the contrary, I assured her that I loved it. She suggested we could go *to the outlet.* I told her I was already a frequent visitor of this establishment, but Louise explained that she was referring to the *family outlet*, one attached to the factory, where only family and employees can go...and rarely the likes of me, she didn't need to add. I was, of course, salivating.

Later, when Abra and I went to the bathroom, she turned to me in awe,

Nita, I think I am the pushiest person around, but you just outdid me!

Several weeks later, Louise escorted me to the factory outside of Florence. I walked in and proceeded to have the ultimate shopping experience - of my life! The venue was as luxurious and elegant as any city centre *Ferragamo* store. Unlike most other outlets I have visited, the clothing is well organized; it's easy to view everything and locate the size you want. Since most of the potential customers were working, we had the place to ourselves. It was quiet, comfortable and the dressing-rooms were beautiful. And the prices! I bought sweaters; a floor length cashmere coat; some classic *Ferragamo* scarves; shoes and boots; and a leather jacket for Montana. All of this for the price of one sweater at the *Ferragamo* store on Rodeo Drive.

Nirvana!

Last year, the outlet Louise introduced to me was opened to the public, but my six years of privileged access gave me some of my happiest shopping moments. Louise was always glad to take me there, while remaining tickled that I thought it was such a big deal. One time, after Tony had moved back to LA, he was coming to spend Christmas with Montana and me in Florence and so I asked her if she would take Tony and me to the outlet to get his Christmas present. Even though she also had family in town, she kindly made time to take us.

Tony had arrived the morning before and was still pretty jet-lagged. Although he's not a big shopping fan, when it comes to buying for him, he's usually game. He's always loved *Ferragamo* shoes and leather goods, so although he had just arrived the day before, even in his exhausted state, he was excited about the trip to the outlet.

This was probably my third or fourth visit. On previous occasions a significant area of the showroom was taken over by men's shoes, clothing and accessories. But when we arrived this time, there was only a single rack for men with a few leather jackets and maybe a dozen pairs of shoes. At six foot, three inches, Tony is much taller and has larger feet than the average Italian man. God bless him, he was like one of Cinderella's evil step-sisters trying to squeeze his foot into one of the handsome shoes. Alas, we quickly realized that there'd be nothing there for him.

Of course, the lack of men's things only meant more space for the women's. There were tons of purses, boots, sweaters, scarves just waiting to be snapped up. It seemed a shame to waste the visit. I was quickly lost in a *Ferragamo* frenzy, buying Christmas gifts for friends and family and, well, yes, one or two things for myself. Meanwhile Tony's jet-lag had gotten the better of him and he'd dozed off on the sofa near the front of the store. Maybe an hour had passed before he opened his eyes to be met with the sight of me, at the cash register, handing over my (our) credit card in exchange for four huge *Ferragamo* bags.

Still a bit dazed from his nap, he looked at Louise, who he knew to be more empathetic with *his* natural frugality rather than *my* somewhat extravagant spending habits. In shock at the scene before him, his head still half in LA, he pipes up,

Great Louise - thanks a lot for my Christmas present!

Collaborazione Blues

Contrary to what you would expect, my partners were never envious that I received the big invitations; met the more famous, influential, and glamorous people; got to do the most interesting interviews; and garnished the greatest attention. Without exception, I asked and encouraged them to accompany me, even wanted them there for both moral and language support. Infrequently did they agree to come along. They were smart; they knew *their* talents and were aware that letting me use *mine* - promoting the paper, selling advertising, getting the big interviews - was what *The Florentine* needed. Giovanni would admonish,

Nita, when you're in the office, you're not working! You need to have meetings all day, you shouldn't be here! (Though I suspect this wanting to get rid of me also had something to do with the way I disturbed the peace in the office.)

Those few times when we were all out together in public, they would point out people that I should talk to and push me in their direction,

He's the owner of the soccer team - go ask him for an interview.

Like an obedient dog, I fetched the bone. Rather than jealousy, I think they were proud of me, and got vicarious pleasure from my insinuation into others' circles and the way I was easily accepted by nearly all the Italians I met.

Though I did spend most of my time out and about, I had many meetings at the office too. I'd get requests to talk to people who wanted to write for us; work for us; advertise with us; volunteer; or do internships. These meetings usually led to enjoyable or informative interactions. I had a more mixed experience with those people who wanted us to write an article *about them*, usually meaning *about their business*. A further group seeking my attention was made up of those who wanted to *collaborate* with us.

When I first heard the word *collaborazione* used in connection with *The Florentine*, I was very interested. It had connotations of *helping* and *sharing* and *mutual benefits*. I saw that we could work with different individuals or organizations on projects that would pay off for everyone. Maybe, by combining resources such as money and access to an audience, we could share costs and deliver more to our readers and advertisers. Or, perhaps we could trade the newspaper's access to readers for business resources we needed to keep the paper up and running.

I soon realized my naïvety on the topic of *collaborazione* in an Italian context. A word that had meant so many positive things throughout my working life became one I would actually grow to hate! What it came to signify to me was: *The Florentine will give you free advertising by writing a positive article on your business* or; *we give you free services like copywriting and translation* or; *I bring my 'rich American' friends and contacts to your place of business* or; *we just give you money because that's what newspapers do* - apparently.

I was astounded by some of the ways these would-be collaborators attempted to get my agreement to either free advertising or some other kind of investment in their business from which it was totally unclear how *The Florentine* would gain. I tried to give the benefit of the doubt, but many of their maneuvers went way beyond shameless attempts at self-promotion and were often thinly veiled ploys to exploit me, my partners and the newspaper.

The approaches came on all fronts and certainly not just from Italians. One day, Giovanni and Linda, our managing editor at the time, insisted I meet with a guy who'd kept calling up and also stopping by the office asking to speak with me - and only me. He was a 50-ish looking American and it was hard not to notice that he was in incredible shape. And the reason for his persistence?

I want to help put The Florentine on the map,

How exactly are you going to do that? I was all ears.

Apparently, this feat was to be achieved by the newspaper sponsoring him while he trained for a bicycle ride around Italy, or to Mecca, or somewhere else I forget now, with the aim of promoting world peace. I asked how exactly his riding a bike was going to achieve this lofty goal, when even more tried and tested methods were currently failing short. He advised me,

Working out how to make that happen is your job; my job is to ride the bike.

Don't get me wrong, I like a bit of *chutzpah* and have been known, at times, to display a little too much of it myself, but this guy pushed the limits. I explained (very politely I thought), that I didn't think it was a good fit for the newspaper, but I wished him luck and would certainly be interested in covering the trip after he reached Mecca or wherever. I thought this would send him on his way. I was not prepared for the guilt trip he started to lay on me,

You have a responsibility as the publisher of The Florentine to make this kind of difference in the world.

I repeated my polite *no* and his response took me by even more surprise,

I'll get you an interview with the Pope.

So, if I didn't help him, I'd be missing the chance to have the interview Diane Sawyer never had! He continued,

You can ask 'him' why the Church collaborated (that word again) *with the Nazis, and why it doesn't use its enormous riches to help the poor.*

This man did something, few people, including Tony, have been able to accomplish: he rendered me (temporarily) speechless. When I could get the words out again, I inquired as to his strategy for getting Nita Tucker from *The Florentine* an audience with Il Papa. Why of course, he enlightened me,

Just by telling him about my bike ride.

How lucky was I that he came to me before Diane, Katie or Oprah?

When I, again, indicated my complete lack of interest, he actually got angry. He informed me I was not the humanitarian I should be and that I was failing to deliver on my duties within the community.

Meanwhile, Giovanni and Linda, who were in the back of the office, had been listening in on the conversation. They were hysterical with laughter when the rejected cyclist made his huffy exit. I was furious with them, especially since I knew they would tease me relentlessly, and for years to come, about my refusing an invitation to interview the Pope.

Another 'opportunity' to collaborate involved a meeting with a musician who was composing, or rather who was *going to* compose, an *extraordinary* opera about Florence. My role was to be the Medici to his Michelangelo, the financier of his genius. My own cash-flow was at best precarious, trying to support myself and the newspaper was sorely testing the elasticity of my credit cards and now here I was being requested to step up as a patron to the arts!

Fortunately, filling *The Florentine* (alas not financing it) was never a challenge. Plenty of useful, interesting and vibrant copy came our way and there was simply no need to use *collaborazione* to create content for the pages. Once I learned my lesson I got smarter at sniffing out ventures that I knew were incompatible with the paper's aims. I became better at heading off, much earlier, offers that were without any obvious advantage to us; that would create an unwelcome financial burden; and, worst of all, in which our involvement could jeopardize the paper's credibility, and therefore our opportunity to make a positive difference for our readers and the local community.

I hated the way that anyone would seek to take me for a *rich, stupid American*. Saying that, I did, occasionally, concur with the *stupid* bit, when, once more, I found myself being sucked in by those enticing words…*we really should collaborate*…

Auguri, Amici and Chocolate Cake Too

I met Jay Mulvaney, a fellow American, and an *Emmy Award* winning writer and producer, at the Ferragamo Museum. He was just leaving as I was about to interview the curator. Jay, who sadly and very prematurely passed away a couple of years ago, was in Florence on a project about which, at first, he was very secretive. I had some ideas though, given that family and celebrity were the topics of his previous books: *Diana & Jackie: Maidens, Mothers, Myths; Jackie: The Clothes of Camelot; and Kennedy Weddings: A Family Album.*

On meeting Jay, I did what I always do when I hear an English-speaker in Florence: I thrust a copy of *The Florentine* in his hand,

Read this, you'll love it!

He returned to the US soon after and later e-mailed to say he had loved it, would soon be returning to Florence for a six week stay and that he would like to meet with me. I pressed him then, via e-mail, on the subject of his project, but met with no response. I wondered if I'd pushed him away with my directness as I never heard back about arrangements to see him.

Having un caffè with Louise Ferragamo one day, she mentioned that an American guy was here and writing about her husband's grandmother, Wanda, wife of the late Salvatore Ferragamo, founder of the family business. I put two and two together and e-mailed Jay. He replied along the lines of,

OK, I'm busted. I'm staying at the Lungarno… but then you probably already know that.

We met up and became good friends - how could we not, he was also a writer, fabulous gossip and celebrity stalker - although, unlike me, he didn't actually need to do so much stalking, already being on first name terms with many celebrities!

I was about to spend my first birthday ever without my family, my second birthday in Florence. I considered the options: feeling sorry for myself or having a party! The latter seemed the only way to go and Jay, with whom I shared my intention, kindly said he'd throw it for me at his apartment in a medieval tower overlooking the Arno. Owned by the Ferragamos, this building also houses their flagship store. When I more than happily accepted his offer, he was straight into interview mode:

Who do you want to invite? What food and drink do you want? What music do you like?

To be honest, despite a lengthy guest list, my only other concern was the cake. Somehow, I've never recovered from my seventh birthday when my mother brought in an elegant, and no doubt very expensive, cake made with marzipan, liquor filling and fruit. Where was the *proper* chocolate birthday cake with the milk chocolate buttercream frosting and the milk chocolate buttercream flowers?

Here is the invite that Jay sent:

Please come for drinks to celebrate the
birthday of our lovely friend
Nita Tucker.
The date is next Thursday, May 3rd
The time is 7:30 - 9:30 (pm, PLEASE don't
surprise me in the morning!)
Regarding gifts:
I happen to know that at the top of her wish list is Sting. A
date, a lunch, an interview, a random sighting on the street, it
matters not - so if anyone can provide Mr. Sumner in the flesh
(CD's don't count), please do. But I also know that running a
close second on her list, and, if you can imagine, even closer to
her heart, is The Florentine. As the paper enters what we Ameri-
cans call the terrible twos, it, like a toddler, is demanding and
expensive. A very special way for us friends to show our love to
Nita is by supporting her baby. Cash is always good, but how
about buying a subscription (or two or three) or taking out an
advertisement, promoting your favorite negozio or cultural
event? The Florentine is moving offices soon, so they will need
many new things: desks, phones, computers, office supplies.
Most important, however, is that this is Nita's first birthday
without her family, so I hope you'll be able to join me as her
FFOC - Florentine-Family-Of-Choice - and celebrate this special
day.

Cheers,
Jay Mulvaney

The invitation was perfect, but then Jay went into a complete *oh-my-God-what-have-I-volunteered-for* panic. He'd no
idea how he was going to give the party, find the food, flowers, drinks, and of course come up with the cake. He called
other friends to his aid. Louise came to the rescue; but then
I always knew that the angels were looking down on me
the day I met her. She has an amazing talent for creatively

dressing spaces and anytime her friends give a party, you'll be sure to find her there an hour before arranging candles, feathers and balloons. So Jay called on Louise to create the party atmosphere.

Also, a couple of days before the party, I got a call from a friend, Ellyn Toscano, then director at Villa La Pietra. I met Ellyn at a *Black and White Ball* hosted by Nora Dempsey at the US Consulate the previous year. Many people had recommended I meet Ellyn to interview her and tour the Villa La Pietra. So when we were introduced, I'd said to her,

You're on my list!

I never did get to interview her, she told me she wanted to have the claim to fame of being the *only* person who stayed on my list. But better than an interview, this beautiful, intelligent and witty woman became my friend. Ellyn has a huge job with responsibilities in Florence and New York, and a young daughter to look after; you can imagine how much spare time she'd have to help organize a friend's party.

Ellyn's call to me went something like this,

I don't know if there's going to be a surprise party for a particular person, but if, hypothetically speaking, there was to be such an event, and if, also hypothetically, there was to be a cake at this event, it had been heard, from some un-named source, that this hypothetical cake had to adhere to strict criteria.

And so I confirmed the necessity of steering well clear of fruit, liquor, and marzipan and the importance of *milk* versus *dark* chocolate. Ellyn continued,

And where, if hypothetically one wanted to buy such a cake in Florence, would one do so?

I didn't know! But undaunted, she asked her final question,

Hypothetically, if there were such a party, and if there were such a cake, how many people would it have to feed?

I invited everyone I knew and that included the many friends I was blessed with and people who I had met or interviewed in a professional capacity, that I liked and wanted the opportunity of getting to know better. When the day came, and I looked around the room I laughed to realize that, to varying degrees, everyone there had been stalked or harassed by me for a *Florentine* related reason. I saw the likes of the talented artist and designer, Patrizia Gucci; my wonderful Ferragamo friends; Aaron Craig and Bari Hochwald from the Florence International Theatre; Contessa Sibilla della Gherardesca, PR executive of Pitti Immagine (which organizes some of the world's biggest fashion events and clothing fairs); Raffaella Antoniazzi from Lungarno Hotels; Barbara Deimling director of Syracuse University; Lily Morghese, director of The Medici Archives; Ellyn Toscano of Villa La Pietra and chocolate cake fame; and, of course, my partners in crime at *The Florentine*.

Auguri!

Seeing this amazing room full of the *who's who* of Florence, smart, confident, beautiful people inside and out, I was in awe that these were now my friends and family in Florence, the people wishing me a happy birthday in my home away from home. Of course, I missed Tony and my children desperately, as well as other equally great friends back in the US, but the sense of belonging, friendship and generosity I experienced, as I cut into my milk chocolate buttercream birthday cake, was overwhelming.

Love Means Never Having to Say You're Sorry?

I had been warned many times about the strong cliquishness I would find in Florence. Florentines I interviewed in my early days advised me to beware of the arrogance and snobbery of most Florentines, before assuring me that they, of course, were not one of these 'provincial' people themselves. I began to think they must be a myth because I never got to meet one of these *snobs*. I soon realized that it was more a case that, being an American, I was outside the social norms and so was less likely to be on the receiving end of any *snobbish* behavior. I was, however, to witness others bearing the brunt of it.

I remember early on in my time with *The Florentine* going to a social event with Marco and Giovanni. We were talking to an acquaintance of mine, or someone who I had interviewed for the paper, and although Marco and Giovanni spoke much better Italian than I did, the person in front of us hardly said a word to them, almost ignoring them. The reason? Marco and Giovanni were Pratesi, from Prato, a town only 20 minutes by car from the center of Florence. Many Florentines look down on the Pratesi...as they do on the Romans, the Sienese, and the Genovese and so on.

This same *looking down* also played out in the business; often advertisers wouldn't even answer Marco's e-mails, only mine. Again, Marco could write and explain things much better to them than I could, but they still preferred to speak with me. It just seemed ridiculous, particularly as Marco is one of the smartest, most well-educated, well-informed, beautifully behaved people I know! He speaks five languages, has traveled the world, knows more things about more subjects than nearly anyone else I can think of: art; film; photography; food; wine; soccer; history; music; furniture design; textiles; architecture. Granted, he's not from Florence, but he's the *real deal* Renaissance man. You'd need to be looking down from pretty high up...

So, as the American and a non-Pratesi member of *The Florentine,* I seemed to take on the role of a mascot. I could cross all lines as *Nita, the American journalist*, or often *Nita, the funny American journalist*. I was hardly judged at all and if I was, it wasn't harshly. The people I needed to interact with to get the job done and the paper out just didn't have a ready conditioned response when it came to dealing with me, however surprised they were on first meeting me. And so, most people, from politicians to princesses, welcomed me into their offices, their palazzos, their families, and their lives.

As to relationships with my partners, after a year of working together, I found out the hard way, that I had truly become *one* of them. We all know the stereotype of the expressive Italian: the anger, hand gesturing, loud arguments and declarations of equally passionate love and hate. For the most part, I found the stereotype exaggerated; I rarely saw strong displays of emotion, even among taxi drivers who, the world over, seem to share a reputation for being open with their opinions and feelings. As to my partners, they also erred on the calmer side of things when going about their business, except that is, when they got angry with each other.

Initially the anger frightened me. I soon understood that the harsh words that were fired off between them, were similar to those of a long married couple; heat of the moment things that would be shouted in the security that they wouldn't lead to an unraveling of a fundamentally committed relationship. When I worked out that this was what was going on, I got less stressed about the occasional show-downs between my Italian partners. Until, that is, I started to find myself at the receiving end...

Marco, in particular, had no problem sending an e-mail informing me that an article was a piece of crap; or that I had no idea what I was doing; or that I wanted to include an article in *The Florentine* just because it was written by a friend; or I had no sense of quality; or a favorite with a high *ouch* rating, that I was killing the newspaper. These attacks came out of nowhere. They were never preceded by his seeking more information to better understand my actions and the intentions behind them. No benefit of the doubt given here.

Giovanni would say similar things to me but with a calmer, more thoughtful, if no less cutting delivery,

Nita, you know that putting in that article was a mistake, or

Perhaps you aren't smart enough to run the paper.

Or even, thank you Giovanni,

You should go back to the States.

As for Leo, although he only yelled or swore at me a couple of times, his words hurt the most. Leo could see how upset I was when this happened and one day he set me straight. He told me that he could never, ever, talk to me in the way he did, if he didn't love me. I knew he was telling me a truth.

There's a notable difference between Italians and Americans talking to each other in such an emotionally charged and seemingly destructive way. In the US, there is a much higher incidence of divorce and also, commonly, many family members are estranged from each other. I know, as do my friends, several people that don't see or talk to their own parents or other relatives and haven't for years. In Italy, this hardly ever occurs - even between childhood friends. On the whole the family bond is much stronger. For both cultural and economic reasons this means that young people stay in the family home longer and, if they do move out, they rarely move beyond the city and still see their family every week. So no matter what is said, how much you hurt another person, you know that they aren't going anywhere, physically or emotionally.

In addition, I discovered that an angry outburst seldom leads to an admission of having said something wrong and certainly not to an apology. I couldn't subscribe to it myself, but a philosophy of *love is never having to say you're sorry* seemed to prevail. Even though I had all this explained to me by Leo and others, who confirmed that such direct attacks truly were an indication of an underlying love and acceptance into the family, it still hurt, devastatingly so. It went against every belief I have about the way people should treat each other and I knew that I'd never get used to it.

I worked mostly with Marco, who was by far the most expressive of the trio, often in positive ways: laughing, hugging, expressing admiration, and performing random acts of kindness. It was also from Marco that I experienced most of, what to me, felt like *attacks*. And so I looked for strategies to take care of myself with him. As things usually kicked off via e-mail, my initial response had been to press reply immediately and send off a defense or justification for whatever I was being so harshly judged. I soon found this generally led to a rapid escalation of emotions on both sides. Next, I tried not responding at all, but this would inflame Marco even further. I experimented with asking Giovanni to speak to him on my behalf; the least successful strategy of all, enough said. Finally I learned to just pick up the phone and almost always, this worked towards some kind of resolution, as did getting together face-to-face.

I never really got used to the hard words. At the same time, I do appreciate that the family is one of Italy's greatest natural resources. I've worked with executives all over the world, and when you ask them their priorities, what is most important to them in life, they all *say* their families. Their *actions*, however, and in particular the amount of time they actually communicate with their nearest and dearest, rarely demonstrate the truth of their words. However, in Italy I found much greater consistency between words and actions when it came to the importance of family.

I feel eternally grateful to have found family myself in Italy; it has been a priceless gift - even when it hurts.

The Da Vinci Touch

Home to a large proportion of the world's art treasures, the city of Florence faces an overwhelming financial challenge in maintaining and restoring them and managing the significant costs of keeping its churches, museums and galleries open to the millions of tourists who come to feast upon all the magnificence. What these art-lovers may not know, is that they have the last descendent of the House of Medici to thank for the fact that such an extensive and priceless collection has remained in Florence.

Anna Maria Luisa de'Medici was, more or less, the last of the dynasty. When she died in 1743, with no heirs of her own, she bequeathed the family's art collection, which included thousands of paintings and sculptures (including the contents of the Uffizi, Palazzo Pitti and Medicean villas) to Florence, on condition that no part of it could be removed from the city. Without her, these riches would have been divided, plundered, sold, the buildings either destroyed or subdivided into condos and hotels.

The legacy of Anna Maria Luisa was generous, but brought with it the many challenges of upkeep. And so, enter stage right, another great woman and present day patron of the arts, Contessa Simonetta Brandolini D'Adda, founder of the *Friends of Florence*. The *Friends* is a non-profit organization with worldwide support which aims to preserve and restore Florentine art in all its forms. This foundation has probably done more for the city's art than any individual or entity since the Medici family, including financing the restoration of many sculptures and paintings, most notably, Michelangelo's *David*. As well as contributing millions of dollars to preserving Florence's incredible artistic heritage for future generations to love and enjoy, the *Friends of Florence* has also funded and organized the documentation of each restoration project, creating beautiful books and films for education and training purposes. By doing so, it has significantly added to Florence's artistic legacy to the world.

Twice a year, Simonetta arranges exclusive cultural itineraries for members of the *Friends*. In the past, these unique events have included cocktails with the *David* himself, in the Academia; private viewings of exhibits in the Uffizi and Vatican, dinners in fairytale castles. *The Florentine* was publishing a book by Professor Rab Hatfield about Leonardo da Vinci's painting, *The Battle of Anghiari,* often referred to as *The Lost Leonardo*. The *Friends* funded the book. To coincide with the publication, Simonetta devoted that year's itinerary to Leonardo. In one of her classically kind gestures, she invited me to join the group for a day in Florence before it headed off for the rest of the trip, which would include a visit to Milan for a private viewing of *The Last Supper* before further events in Paris.

In the Salon de Cinquecento of the Palazzo Vecchio, the day began with the scholars on the committee searching for *the Lost Leonardo* showing us the Vasari frescoes under which they believe this work can be found. Rab explained the research that had led them to this conclusion. Maurizio Seracini, a notable character and well renowned art authenticator also involved in this intriguing search (mentioned, as himself, in Dan Brown's *The Da Vinci Code*), gave us a discourse on the complex engineering techniques that he and others are developing to reveal, and finally confirm, the location of *The Battle of Anghiari*.

Afterwards, we took a slight detour from the Leonardo theme to visit an ongoing project being funded by the *Friends*. We went to the laboratory where three imposing sculptures (twice actual life size and normally on display in the Baptistery), by the great Renaissance artist Giovanni Francesco Rustici, were being restored. Rustici was a contemporary of Leonardo's and it is believed they shared lodgings at the time he was working on these magnificent bronzes of *John the Baptist with the Pharisee and the Levite*. The restorers educated us about their special techniques. They explained the difficult decisions they had to make to achieve the overall best outcome, needing to take precautions to ensure they did not over-restore or even further damage these unique and impressive pieces.

We lunched at a villa outside Florence, the home of an Italian board member of the *Friends*, who shared with us his eclectic collection of both Italian masters and contemporary art. The villa's gardens were breathtaking. Our lunch was served with a fine selection of Frescobaldi wine. Now, there's a life to which I could become accustomed.

Alas, I had to miss the next part of the day, a visit to one of my favorite museums in Florence, the Bargello, a former barracks and prison that now houses the largest Italian collection of gothic and Renaissance sculpture. Work was calling me back to the office, but wild horses were not going to prevent me from rejoining the group for its evening activities. After its doors were closed to the general public, I headed for the Uffizi, once more delighting in the privileges that my time and work at *The Florentine* were affording me. I knew, with my name on the select list of those allowed entry, that I was going to see something extraordinary.

The public rooms of the iconic Uffizi Gallery, said to house 40% of the artistic treasures of the world, are quite something in themselves, and even more so after hours. Yet we were taken, to somewhere even more special, a room which is never open to the public. The curator's formal black dress and breathtaking emerald and diamond necklace, added to the aura of importance surrounding the occasion. Fortunately, I too was suitably dressed in black (as I always am); alas my glitter was paste. She slowly pulled on her white gloves and, should we have been in any doubt, emphasized that *few people have ever seen what you are about to see.* The room was hushed as she opened a portfolio and took out a Leonardo. There were gasps. Before our eyes, was Leonardo's only landscape drawing; in pencil - clear, clean, fresh, as though recently drawn.

Gary Radke, the professor leading the *Friends of Florence* on its entire five day trip, remarked that, when teaching, he often used slides of this particular landscape but had never seen the original and had been quite unprepared for the power of the experience. The overall impression of the piece, the way the subject was captured, in itself brought vitality to this drawing, but it was something else that reminded me that, at the end of the day, this was the work of a real man, albeit a talented genius. It was the sight, afforded by our close viewing, of the individual strokes on the paper that was so moving. I could visualize Leonardo's hand resting on the paper, making each of the single marks that would form the whole. There was something very intimate about seeing these so closely with the naked eye. We also viewed pencil studies of a drapery, the shadows showing Leonardo's mastery of light and dark. And there was a drawing of a woman, angelic, nymph-like, not of this world.

I felt weak at the knees.

We left these treasures to view the three Leonardo paintings which form part of the Uffizi's permanent collection. I'd been in this gallery many times, but being there with just 30 people, with no time limit, the sensors switched off so that we could approach each work of art closely, was a very different experience. Gary directed our attention to where the studies we had just seen had been incorporated into the paintings we now viewed. The elements of these drawings were brought further to life in these magnificent oils.

The group with which I shared this experience was made up of some very knowledgeable, sophisticated, and wealthy American contributors (and me!). Many had the means and access to similarly privileged experiences amidst the artistic wonders of the world and had *been there* and *done that* in a very impressive way. Yet, I was not surprised to see that no one seemed jaded by these previous experiences, no one immune to the unique advantage they had just been gifted - everyone had been visibly moved by what they had seen that evening.

Dinner, surely, would be an anti-climax.

We went to the cafeteria of the Uffizi which we discovered had been dramatically transformed from its daytime appearance. The long table was ready to seat us all; lit by candlelight and laden with flowers, linens, crystal and silver, all worthy of the unique setting. We took our places. One wall of windows looked out onto the illuminated Duomo and the magnificent towers of Palazzo Vecchio. Fascinating dinner conversation was interrupted by short operatic interludes. Tuxedoed waiters with white gloves brought exquisite food and Antinori wine.

At the stroke of midnight, I did my Cinderella number, though with the aid of a bicycle rather than a pumpkin carriage. My 'jewels' and gown put to rest, I call my far away prince to recount my day, to confirm this dream had actually been a reality, before my cheek hits the pillow.

With Friends Like These...

Channel surfing while in Italy, I caught the headline on Sky TV: *Amici*. I assumed it was a dubbed version of the US series *Friends*, or maybe the Italian adaptation of the popular show. As it turned out *Amici* couldn't have been more unlike *Friends* if it had been titled, *Enemies*. Uniquely Italian, it's a hugely popular reality show screened seven days a week. One February, I had the opportunity to travel to Rome and experience the *Amici* phenomena first hand with a view to writing an article for *The Florentine*.

Amici is filmed at Cinecittá, the iconic studio which is considered the home of Italian cinema. It was built by Benito Mussolini as a critical element of his propaganda drive: *Il cinema e l'arma piu forte* he declared...*cinema is the most powerful weapon*. The Western Allies bombed Cinecittá in WWII but it lived to fight another day becoming most closely associated with Federico Fellini, whose blend of fantasy and baroque created movies that attracted world attention.

Today Cinecittá is still very much in use, for both TV and film production, despite overcoming, amongst other challenges, near bankruptcy in the 80s and a big fire in 2007. However, unlike anything I'd experienced on visits to its Hollywood counterparts such as Paramount and Universal, as I entered the gates I had an eerie sense of stepping back in time. I was instantly transported to the scenes of *La Dolce*

Vita. Maybe I was falling down a rabbit hole into a Fellini film?

The need for a quick bite before the filming of *Amici* started snapped me out of my reverie and I headed to the cafeteria with my hosts only to have the frozen-in-time experience intensified. A woman came up to our table. She was 60, 70, or maybe 102. I thought she was a waitress about to clear the table; an old woman, doing an ordinary job. And yet there was something unnerving about her presence as she stood there staring at us. With her strange aura and a huge and hairy mole on her chin, repulsive and yet compelling, she verged on the sinister. She made no attempt to clear the table and instead, after an awkward silence, announced that she was an actress and, presumably prompted by the American accents she had heard, she instructed,

Take me back to Hollywood with you.

My friend leaned over and whispered that the woman was indeed an actress; she had, in fact, appeared in every Fellini film. While she didn't work in the cafeteria, she was always there, maybe living somewhere on the lot. Perhaps, went the stories, she was the ghost of a long-ago spurned starlet, or an apparition peeled away from the celluloid, able to come to life, but only within the confines of the Cinecittá lot.

We left the woman behind, but the surreal continued as we entered the studio, an amphitheatre filled with a roaring and stomping crowd, whose soundtrack could have easily been used for a gladiatorial combat scene in a Roman epic. Maybe there was a mix-up, the recent series *Rome* was filmed here; there were no togas in sight but maybe we'd stumbled into a rehearsal. The audience was doing a very passable imitation of the plebeians baying for Christians, lions and blood. The flashing lights and ever-increasing volume of the music, however, made it clear in which century we actually were. The decibels rose yet further as the time approached for the filming of *Amici* to start. If only I'd appreciated, in my discomfort, that this lively warm-up was the part I was going to enjoy the most. Deafened, I thought about going back to the cafeteria for a quiet chat and un caffé with the Cinecittá ghost; she was seeming less sinister by the moment.

An attempt to explain the basics of *Amici:* it's similar to *American Idol*, a young people's talent contest with competitors seeking the prize of a professional contract. Like *Idol*, *Amici* holds auditions for the thousands of hopeful 18-25 year olds looking for a place on this highly rated national show, currently in its ninth season. The two dozen performers that make it through the auditions are then divided into two opposing teams which come to Cinecittá to live and take classes in singing, acting and dancing for four to six hours a day, alongside their fellow team-mates.

The only time the *opposing* teams meet is to compete on Saturday and Sunday evenings when Maria de Filippi, the producer and pretty much the boss, a powerful woman in Italian television, appears as host of the show and announces the participants and the theme of the competitions. These selections are made when she turns her back to the audience and looks at a large flashing screen, the lights passing across the performers' names and various singing, dancing and acting possibilities. The lights stop, the audience go wild, the contenders and an event are revealed: a team to perform a certain style (ballet, jazz, tango) of dance; a couple to act a short scene; or an individual to sing a solo. Each performance is critiqued by a panel of 'experts'.

These judges included a singer, an over-the-top drag queen and an over-the-hill ballerina. In comparison, their post-performance comments made *Idol's* Simon Cowell seem like a protective and encouraging uncle. Their duties also included being the participants' teachers throughout the week. The ballerina judge, her *stabbing-you-in-the-back* tone unmistakable, informed the girl she'd been training and mentoring,

Don't feel bad that you're not a good dancer, because some people are just not cut out for it.

But this, and more overtly cutting criticism, is not just confined to the judge-contestant relationship; the judges are equally enthusiastic about throwing flames at each other. On this occasion the singing teacher accused the ballerina *maestra* of jealousy and bitterness now that she was no longer a star, declaring that she was using the show merely as a vehicle for her self-promotion. Duh! Why else is someone likely to appear on a show like this? This wasn't merely friendly banter, it was vicious, lasting many minutes and, I soon realized, an integral part, if not the *point*, of the program.

Such sadistic repartee between the judges, however, provided a mere *snack* for the hungry spectators, whose booing and screaming left you in no doubt with which judges and contestants their sympathies rested. The *real meal* came when the teams themselves got to critique their fellow performers - or should that be castigate, denigrate, and annihilate them? This unpleasant exercise began with the showing of video clips, shot during the week, of the participants talking behind each others' backs. The montage was edited to include only cruel, nasty, fierce and hate-filled comments directed at individuals of the opposing team. Then, live, the cameras zoomed in on the target of the never-nice comments with he or she being asked how it felt to hear them. The host then encouraged further attacks and counter-attacks, most of which were personal, having nothing to do with the performances or the talents of the contenders. The nastier it all gets, the more frenzied the audience becomes; and the more frenzied the audience becomes, the higher, it seems, the ratings get.

Coming from the world of *Big Brother, Fantasy Island, and Fear Factor,* it's not like I'm claiming any moral high ground for my nation's TV, but I was pretty appalled by the way that *Amici* exploited people at such a vulnerable age. The rabid response of the audience, and the spotlight given to the nastiest comments and most back-stabbing of behaviors, had the effect of rewarding these young people for excelling at treating people in a way that no culture, that I know of, supports or condones, in people of any age. Yes, tough love and hard words are given on *American Idol,* but at least the judges are independent to those who have been teaching, mentoring and supporting the participants. From what I've seen of *Idol,* the competition takes people on a journey of learning and growth and this blossoming of confidence and talent is, in my opinion, inspirational to watch. Also, the ethos of the contest is self-improvement not destruction of your fellow competitors. No, I'm not about to recommend Simon Cowell for sainthood, and I'm no Pollyanna either; I'm sure there's gossip and bitching behind the scenes of *Idol* and similar programs, I just doubt that it's as actively encouraged, if encouraged at all, and certainly it's not so obviously and publically fuelled and rewarded in the interests of ratings.

On *Amici,* what *is* given the most attention, screen time and applause is *not* the entertainment provided by the skill and talent of the young people (it's even hard to recall who performed what and how good they were amongst all the hoopla) but, instead, the contestants honing the art of being hurtful and vile to each other. Of course this says as much about the audience as the performers, both in the studio and at home watching on TV.

Long after the death of the great Fellini, the dark and grotesque live on at Cinecittá. And not just in the cafeteria.

Shana Tova: A Miracle in Florence

It was fast approaching *Rosh Hoshanah*, widely known as the Jewish New Year. From the time I was a child, (and I know I'm not alone amongst others of my faith) it was only the *High Holidays* that had me heading for the synagogue. In Florence, such times were another opportunity for Marco and me to clash.

I'd want to get the times of the special services printed in the newspaper. Marco's frustration was that we already had the schedule of regular weekly religious services included in the *Important Numbers* page. I tried to explain how important it was to highlight *High Holiday* services for the English speaking Jews in Florence,

It would be like an Italian Catholic in Egypt on December 24th not knowing where to attend mass and at what time the service started!

He still thought it was ridiculous and unnecessary. But, however last minute it was, I always made sure the details were boxed and highlighted in the paper.

I'd describe my upbringing as *culturally*, rather than *religiously* Jewish. My own spiritual journey has been, and I realize I'm far from unique in this, an exploration of varied beliefs and philosophies mixing political, social and religious thinking. The phases have been many: beatnik; radical; hippie; pop psychologist; transcendental meditation student; Tai Chi practitioner; and follower of Zen and Tibetan

Buddhism. While the journey continues, it's perhaps slowed its pace a little. An interesting turn of events happened when I arranged for my son, Jordan, to prepare for his *Bar Mitzvah*, a decision made without hesitation on my part and with my non-Jewish husband's full support. It was at this time I realized that, for all my spiritual investigation, I knew very little about the beliefs and traditions of what was still essentially, my own religion.

I signed up for an introduction to Judaism class aimed at those actually converting into the faith. And so at 51, as a result of what I'd learned, I was inspired to take my *Bat Mitzvah*, the female equivalent of what is more widely viewed as a male tradition. One of the strongest memories I have of this day is the sense of serenity and power that came with reading Hebrew, a special hard to describe feeling, almost a vibration, resulting from chanting an ancient language aloud. I've heard people say this about reading Sanskrit.

I am far from being an orthodox Jew; *reform* would be the nearest description of my faith. I don't observe the Sabbath in full, or keep to a kosher diet, but I am drawn to many of Judaism's traditions and teachings. Now, in LA, I attend, most Saturdays, the inspiring services of Rabbi Mordecai Finley at Ohr Ha Torah Synagogue. A non-Jewish friend, an atheist actually, attended a service where I read the Torah as part of my birthday celebrations. She was blown away by the joy of it all and, in particular, the Rabbi's Torah study session, always thought-provoking explorations into living a good life, with relevance whatever your beliefs.

For *Rosh Hoshanah* during my second year in Florence, I wanted to seek out a service that, to some extent at least, reflected my own version of my Jewish faith. I didn't want to go to the main synagogue because although a resplendent place, I knew I wasn't looking for the kind of service that would be held there - orthodox, all in Hebrew, with the women separated in an upper balcony behind bars. Basically, it would be hot, stuffy and I'd be too far from the action for my liking.

I'd learned about a group of Italians and ex-pats who'd started holding progressive Jewish services in a classroom of a local school. I'd made sure their schedule for the *High Holidays* was in the paper alongside those of the main synagogue. I decided to attend myself and on *Rosh Hoshanah* morning I rode my bike to the school. There were maybe 25 people in the room and a small ark, holding a single Torah. We sat on plastic chairs surrounded by schoolwork and blackboards. We were greeted in Italian, by Stefano, who explained that sadly the man who was supposed to blow the *shofar*, the ram's horn, which forms a significant part of the proceedings, wasn't able to come because a friend of his had died the night before. He asked, surely in vain, if anyone amongst us knew how to play the *shofar* and could step in.

The group was made up of several tourists, who'd heard about the services from our paper or their concierge, a handful of Italians, a few ex-pats and a couple of US exchange students. We looked around at each other and were surprised when a young American girl from Washington DC, traveling in Florence with her parents, raised her hand and said that she did. She must have been in her early twenties and I looked at her, thinking maybe she'd once picked up a *shofar* at religious school. I imagined her skill level to be something similar to mine on a kazoo!

Absent of a rabbi, Stefano led the service; in *real life*, he was a psychologist. He spoke very little English, so a friend of his translated. We all performed the service together; he asked different people to read the various parts and we pitched in to read Hebrew, or English or Italian. We discussed the *parshah*, the portions of text, in a mixture of Italian and English. At one point Stefano forgot an *aliyah*, the prayer to be said before he started the next *parshah* and we knew to remind him. No one was scheduled to do anything, but it all got done. For the last *aliyah*, the entire congregation came forward to stand at the Torah. At this point a friend next to me remarked upon the bad cold from which I was obviously suffering; not a very close friend or she'd have instantly understood that the tears streaming down my face were the result of something else entirely.

My emotion was a response to the overwhelming awe of the experience. I was thinking back to my *Bat Mitzvah*. Up until my son Jordan's *Bar Mitzvah*, I'd always thought of this ceremony as a rite of passage, a boy becoming a man. But I learned it is the time that a boy, or girl, takes on the responsibility for continuing the Jewish religion. I had come to this responsibility later in life, experiencing the joy and honor of knowing how to read the Torah, and how to lead a Shabbat service. I looked around the room, a witness to the success of this plan for continuity. What exactly was it, I wondered, that had driven this otherwise unrelated group of Jews to attend this service? How, after thousands of years, did this still continue? When I grew up in Detroit we went to services, I thought, simply because everyone did, all my friends and family were Jewish. In Florence, most of my friends were Italian, and even amongst the ex-pats, I only knew two Jewish families. What, I wondered, had made me carve out this time from my own life to be here with these people, mostly strangers, and to join in this service to spiritually prepare for the New Year?

Then, the time came for the blowing of the *shofar*. The volunteer came to the front, a little embarrassed and apologizing because she was 13 when she'd last performed the task, so maybe I was right about the religious school. We would have been grateful for a mere sound; instead, we heard the varied responses at the appropriate times - long, broken or staccato notes. She blew to symbolically awaken us from our slumbers, alert us to the coming judgment and remind us that *God is King.*

She was magnificent.

The week following the service, and at many times since, I've connected this experience in my head to the story of *Chanukah*, when we celebrate the miracle of the oil that was only enough for one day and lasted eight. Jewish from birth, I know a lot of Jewish people, friends, family, neighbors, teachers, colleagues. Not one of them knows how to blow the *shofar* and at all the different services I've attended over the years, it was always an older man who blew it.

On hearing this story, a friend told me that she'd read that the person who blows the *shofar* on *Rosh Hashanah* should: *be learned in the Torah and shall be God-fearing; the best man available. Nevertheless, every Jew is eligible for any sacred office, providing he is acceptable to the congregation.* (Shulchan Aruch 3:72.) Who would have thought that a young, hip, beautiful, American girl, in Florence for just a couple of days, would turn out to be our very acceptable choice?

The event was a New Year miracle.

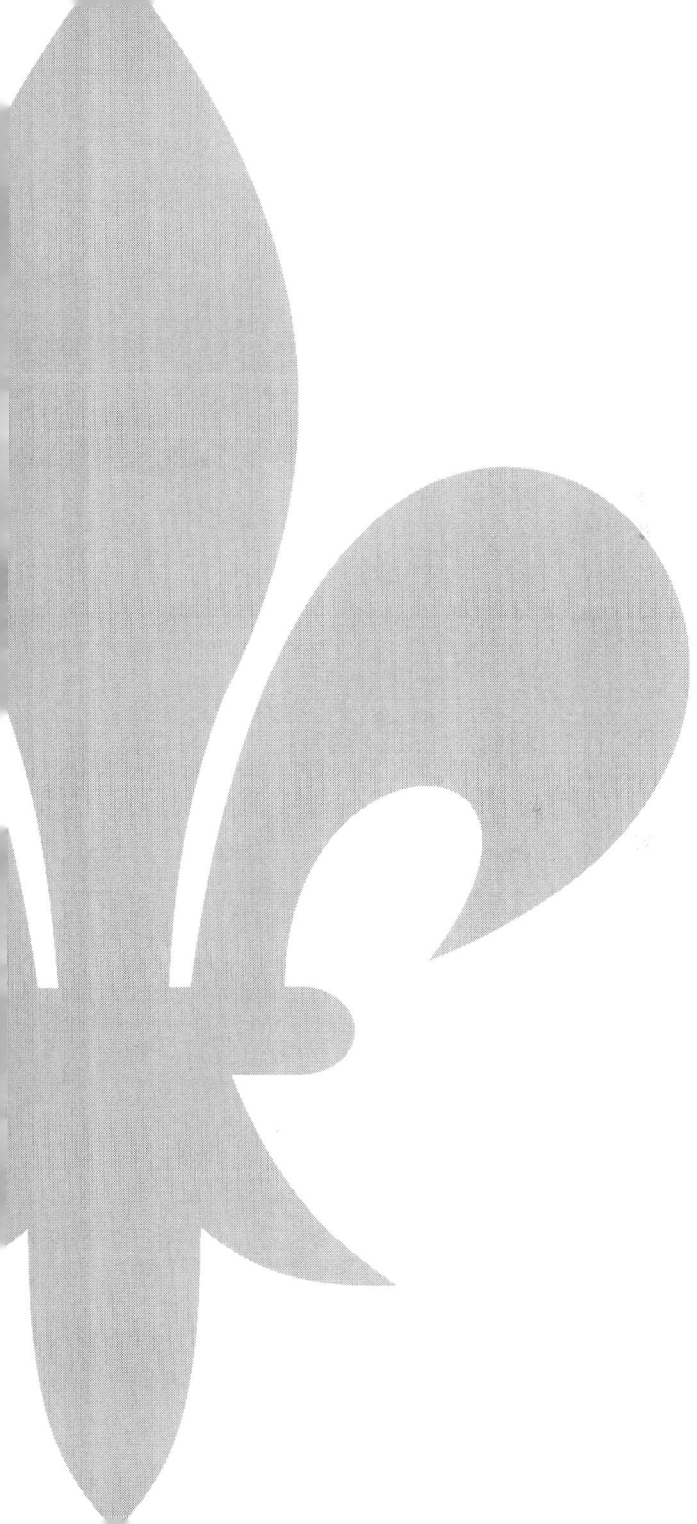

If the Pheasant Plucker Could Pluck Pheasants... Would He?

One Sunday after a weekend at Il Borro, as guests of Louise and Jamie Ferragamo, I was getting into the car to leave, when Jamie ran up to me with two huge *Ferragamo* bags. Clothes? Boots? A purse? I opened them and peered excitedly inside - somewhat disappointed to see the plumes of a considerable number of dead pheasants! Jamie had obviously thought ahead to any objections I may have presented,

For your Thanksgiving dinner - to serve alongside the turkey.

I remembered my manners,

Thanks a lot Jamie.

Now, my friends would be nothing short of alarmed if they thought I'd actually be cooking a Thanksgiving dinner myself; I'd immediately allayed any fears by hiring a chef. I've never even cooked a chicken if the truth be told, let alone a turkey, or a pheasant! It seemed the obvious thing to do was to let the chef know about this new addition to the planned menu. Her only question,

Are they plucked?

Jamie is extremely generous and indeed, multi-talented, but no, I explained, he'd not plucked the pheasants before he'd handed them over. She, in turn, enlightened me that there was no way she could prepare the birds by Thursday;

that plucking was a process that took about three hours per pheasant and; it was a nasty job that included steaming, heavy labor, a stinky house and usually, personal injury in the form of cuts to the palms and fingers. It was a task traditionally carried out on the country estates by the *contadini,* farm workers. She had heard, however, that there were some machines outside of town that you could hire to help get the job done.

Not ready to give up, I said I'd go to Sant' Ambrogia market the next day and ask around. I went to *Cibreo* for my morning cappuccino and showed Isadoro, my barista, the treasures inside my *Ferragamo* bags. He was extremely impressed, informing me that a great delicacy was in store for me. I asked him if he knew someone who could pluck them, and to my surprise, he instructed,

Ask a policeman.

His suggestion was based on some recently introduced laws, connected to this kind of dirty work. Leaving the café I was fortunate to bump into an Italian couple I knew, whose daughter was in school with Montana. They happily came with me to the market to talk to the different butchers there, and also to inquire of a policeman. The latter idea, they advised me, was *insane.* I loved the way that, in Italy, when people claim superior knowledge on a matter this renders everyone else's ideas and suggestions as not merely *wrong,* but *ridiculous, stupid, naïve,* or best of all, *a plain lie!*

We talked to many butchers who kept sending us to other vendors in the market; several of which had no obvious pheasant-connection, the scarf lady for example. However, this woman did turn out to be an occasional poultry-plucker. My rising hopes were dashed when she said she wouldn't be able to make my Thursday deadline due to a prior engagement requiring her to deprive someone else's birds of their feathers!

Although lacking success, we were thoroughly entertained by the varied conversations. I was repeatedly told how lucky I was to have such beautiful birds; how tasty they would be; what work it would take to prepare them; that I should undertake the job myself; and with what wine I should serve with the wonderful *fagiani*. Many had a good laugh at the suggestion to speak to a policeman, including the policeman we asked. It was a very enjoyable morning, but alas, I walked back home with the same two sorry bags of pheasants getting heavier by the minute…and no solution.

I resigned myself to a pheasant-less Thanksgiving.

Later that day I went into the office, birds still in hand so to speak, and showed them to one of my Italian associates working on the paper. She was delighted to take them off me and said she would have *The Florentine* staff over to her house for the feast the following week. She took a day off from work and spent hours preparing the meal. In Italy, good food is something to be honored; the *fagiani* being considered as special, there was an obligation to prepare them well. And there was me on the verge of throwing them away!

It was the first time I had tasted the dark, obviously gamey, bird; served alone as the *secondi* after a *primi* course of polenta. It was, at least, after all the effort, an outstanding meal. My gift from Jamie was honored in the end. However, I wasn't sure I'd be as quick to take a couple of *Ferragamo* bags off him in the future.

What's Not to Like?

It's easy to romanticize about Italy; that's why many people do. There's so much that can be said about...so much: the food and wine; the art, fashion and architecture; the warmth and humor of the people; the piazza-life with its caffé and gelato; the closeness of the family; its complex and illustrious history. No wonder so many of us ex-pats want to learn Italian, live *under the Tuscan sun*, become one of the locals, and look down on the ugly, uncultured and yes, in many cases horribly dressed and overweight Americans who stand out in the crowds of tourists.

The more Italians I met through work and social activities and making my way in Florence, and the more I learned about their culture and way of life, the richer my own life became. Yet, I never forgot that it was my American gutsiness, courage, and sense of adventure that got me to my beloved Florence in the first place, not to mention the *chutzpah* it took to make *The Florentine* happen. And, I also had a few harder lessons to learn about life in my new home.

Despite the many, many glorious things, there were a few aspects of Italian culture that I soon realised I would never fully embrace. Some of these were mere frustrations and could even be the source of amusement, the confusion of road signs and shop opening times, for example. Others, I would on no account find funny and gave me insights into a way of thinking for which my admiration and respect would never be forthcoming, however long I was to live in Italy. These included some characteristics not necessarily exclusive to Italians, nor witnessed in the behavior of every Italian I met, but which I did come up against frequently in my life and work on *The Florentine*.

Something that caused me endless dismay was the admiration that was given to those who were considered *furbo come una volpe* - sly like a fox. A person labeled as *furbo*, I soon discovered, was being applauded for being smart enough *to get away with it*, irrespective of the lies by omission; failure to bring to attention an honest mistake; or more active deceit or cheating, that had been employed with the aim of taking advantage of another. Viewing such behaviors as something to be admired goes totally against my own values around fairness and integrity. I also didn't see this as a good business practice; to me *furbo* was just plain short-sighted as it reduced the opportunity to build trusting relationships with lasting benefits.

There were other aspects of how *furbo* was valued that I found challenging too. For instance, if someone with whom you were doing business made an error that worked in your favour such as quoting less for some work through a miscalculation, it would be considered a sign of weakness, if not the height of stupidity, if you were to helpfully point out what he or she had done. And further, if you'd been a victim of *furbo*, God forbid that you'd expect any empathy or consolation for being actively duped or more quietly taken advantage of. If you are then *che schemo!* Others would see that you've had your just desserts for your own stupidity - and kudos to the sneaky con artist for taking the opportunity to move in on someone so shockingly naïve.

Most disturbing was seeing instances of how this 'value' was encouraged in children. I was amazed when, one day, I overhead a mother saying in response to her daughter's suggestion that they clean up the poop their dog had just deposited,

No, we don't have to, no one is looking.

Such was my distaste for this and other conventions of *furbo* that they were often the cause of many disagreements between me and my Italian partners. Information I would choose to make transparent to others, was seen as a sign, not of my doing *the right thing*, but of my own inexperience around sound business practice. This would particularly frustrate me when the guys refused to believe that anyone writing a business related story for *The Florentine*, or any story mentioning a restaurant or hotel, was not doing so because they were getting a kick-back for it. Even the professional English and American journalists who contributed to the paper, and had, to me, such an obvious reason never to risk their reputation were, according to partners, taking payments to write nice words. I was considered beyond naïve for my ignorance of this 'fact'.

I firmly believe that being honest, fair and open is how to get ahead, in all aspects of life, and definitely in business; these beliefs brought me much ridicule from my Italian partners who thought me a true innocent with no sense of how to conduct myself properly in these matters. The fact that I'd provided leadership and management consultancy to many highly successful global corporations, the likes of Cisco, Hewlett-Packard, Motorola and Xerox, was incredulous to them, to the point where I'm not sure that they really believed that I had.

One time, Giovanni complimented me on an editorial I had written. He seemed surprised that I had worded it so well. I responded,

You know, Giova, you are shocked that I do something well, but major corporations actually hire me to consult. In fact, they even pay me a lot of money.

He looked at me with his *how stupid* look that at first I thought was a comment about me, but then it registered,

Oh my God, you think that they must be idiots to pay that kind of money for me?

He nodded. He certainly had no idea *how much* they actually paid for my consultancy and had he done so, maybe I would have earned his respect; surely this would show me to be *molto-furba* for duping these industry leaders into parting with such large sums of cash!

Another issue which raised its head when working on *The Florentine,* again a major challenge to my own beliefs and values, was my colleagues' attitudes toward *the competition.* To them, people who worked in the same industry were - *obviously* - enemies. For me, competition at its best is exemplified in the Olympics: the better the opponent does, the better you have to be to beat them. The impossible keeps becoming possible; boundaries are crossed and records broken; excellence and mastery get completely redefined every four years. Although people want to win, they want to win against their opponent's best game. A win doesn't taste as sweet when it comes as a result of someone else getting injured, an unheroic trip, or a disqualification.

My approach, shared I know with many others, is to honor the competition, not least of all because they make you have to perform better, pushing you to raise the bar. I've been friends with real and potential competitors, and I never wish anything but the best for them. My experience in Italy was of another way of dealing with the competition: disparaging, belittling and offering insults were all considered acceptable behaviors towards it. Being outwardly thrilled by examples of its poor performance was also entirely permissible.

Friendship with the competition, I was soon to learn, was not seen *appropriate* for my role with *The Florentine*. The way that other magazines (given that we were the only local newspaper) and journalists were discussed in the office, made me see that reaching out to explore joint ventures would be deemed complete madness. As for people who had left *The Florentine* and moved on to do other things, people for whom my partners had once seemed to have the utmost respect, they were suddenly not to be trusted and their competence called into question. My suggestion that we continue to use a particular individual who'd taken up a role doing events with another periodical was met with complete derision, even though she was all but volunteering her, previously considered very competent, services.

When discussing this Italian *imperfection* (as I saw it), with my friend Pino, a dancer, who had been part of several US dance troupes and so lived away from Italy for many years, he explained,

You have to remember, Nita, Italy is the home of Machiavelli and for many, his is still the philosophy by which they live. Do you know that even doctors will rarely consult each other for a second opinion?

In this regard I did not care to, nor would I, emulate Italians. I'd go out of my way to connect people that I knew, because of this attitude towards the competition, wouldn't do so of their own accord, happily seeing the positive outcomes. Getting two respected and prominent female chefs together at a meal was a great win on this front, as was getting together women who had key roles with some of Florence's major hotels and design houses.

I'm regularly asked to speak to students studying in Florence at *Polimoda*, the International Institute of Fashion (which is affiliated with FIT in New York), to help orient them for the duration of their studies. I share my own experience and thinking about adjusting to, and embracing, a life in Florence,

It's easy to complain about things in Italy. Yes, it takes five times longer to get anything done; it's hard to get service; the signage confuses or isn't even there in the first place; and shop opening hours are cruelly unpredictable. But, if these things are important to you, my counsel is to stay home. I made a decision early on, especially when I was regularly hopping between two continents, that when I was in Italy, I wouldn't complain about how it was not like the US; and when in the US, I wouldn't complain about it not having the charm, great food, and 'feel' that I loved so much about Italy.

One of my favourite needlepoint homilies is,

Love is: loving a person the way he is and the way he is not.

And I'd apply the same to loving a culture, or a city, or a country. At the end of the day, if the good things outweigh the not-so-good ones then we tend to be happy. And so it was with me and Italy. I chose to make Florence my home and yes, there were things I found challenging, but it was clear that the good and often wondrous things that I experienced on a daily basis more than compensated for those aspects of life with which I struggled. Whatever decisions we make in life, whether about where to live; or to which people we'll give time, energy and love; or even how we opt to make a living, there'll be both positive outcomes and downsides that result from our choices. While I would clearly never come to value *furba* or act towards my business competition as if it were the enemy, I'm still very able to love Florence: *for the way she is... and the way she is not.*

Punching the Clock

Some weeks I'd have to pinch myself to be sure that my role with the newspaper was actually my job. OK, so I wasn't actually getting a salary, but the other currencies that came my way were numerous (and some of the experiences priceless). The way my working life and social life seamlessly weaved together was particularly satisfying for me. If I was interviewing someone, or visiting somewhere for an article, it would never feel as if I was *on the job* - and often the people and places I discovered on 'days off' led to features for *The Florentine*. In one way I never felt *at work* but, in another, I never felt *off-duty*.

The beginning of what turned out to be a particularly eventful week began when I accompanied Daniel, one of our interns at *The Florentine* and a law student at NYU (taking a semester to study at the European University Institute in Florence), to interview one of his professors. The professor in question, somehow finding the time to keep up with his original teaching career, was the then Minister of the Interior for Italy, Giuliano Amato. In former days he had twice been Italian Prime Minister.

Amato has a nickname: *Dottor Sottile,* which means both *Dr Thin* and *Dr Subtilis,* cleverly referring to both his slight physical appearance and his reputation for the nuances of his political insight. We met him in his small office at the EUI in San Domenico. I told him I was honored to meet him,

It's no honor, he humbly replied.

The Minister of the Interior's portfolio is similar to that of Homeland Security in the US. Daniel asked about the considerable challenges his position presented. Amato explained that, in addition to a variety of internal security issues, his role primarily focused on two things: immigration and terrorism, managing the former and preventing the latter. He saw danger in the fact that the public commonly linked these two phenomena while, in fact, he viewed them as having nothing at all to do with each other.

Amato's small physical presence had in no way limited the stature and respect he's gained as a leader. I was intrigued as to how he coped with the responsibilities of his position,

What's it like to be a world leader, to wake up in the morning with the task of keeping Italy safe from terrorism?

He shared that, yes, he often felt the weight of his duties and the challenge of dealing with things he could not personally control, but, though difficult, it was rewarding work.

Daniel went on to ask him about his academic career. He explained that he saw himself as born to be a professor, not a politician, and that his teaching may well prove to be the biggest contribution he makes in life. I could see his obvious joy when he described his passion for teaching and the impact of seeing the *light turn on* for his students when they learned something that opened their minds and challenged, and often changed, something they had previously believed. Witnessing this experience, he admitted, brought a feeling of satisfaction way beyond that which came with having a statute passed in parliament.

I was struck by how, well, normal, I found Giuliano Amato. He wasn't outwardly charismatic but at the same time didn't come across as falsely humble or self-effacing. I can't remember who said it, or even the exact words, but something came to my mind about *heroes not being extraordinary people, but ordinary people who have extraordinary commitments.*

Afterwards, reflecting on our 30 minutes with the Minister, I thought of a dinner party I'd attended a few days earlier. Among the others guests, was President George Bush's uncle, brother to George H. Bush. In Italian there are two different words meaning *you* - one to be used formally and one informally. Obviously with the Minister I used the formal, more polite term. If it wasn't unsettling enough to find myself sitting down to eat with a Bush family member, I found it further odd the way he presented himself to me, extending his hand to shake and introducing himself,

Hi, I'm Buck Bush. (I had to ask him to repeat himself, because I had heard a similar sounding phrase so many times in those years of his nephew's presidency!)

A few days later I headed to Rome with Alexandra, *The Florentine's* managing editor at the time. Our first stop was the American Academy. I'd long heard this place described as *a haven of creativity* and knew that being awarded the *Rome Prize* by the American Academy gave artists and scholars the opportunity to pursue their work and studies in a very special environment. This respected institution was created in 1913 by the merger, in Rome, of the American School of Architecture and the American School of Classical Studies. Vanderbilts, Rockerfellers and Carnegies all had a hand in its creation and development. I thought the place would make a great article for *The Florentine,* a perfect merger of the American and the Italian.

Even though we were led to expect something quite special, Alex and I were still awestruck by the beauty and refined atmosphere of the Academy's setting on Gianicolo, one of the hills of Rome. It made for a splendid sanctuary for artists and scholars, exquisite gardens providing a tranquil place for reflection and inspiration, all with a view of one of the world's grandest cities. At a more practical level, every meal is prepared for the *Rome Prize* recipients with menus supervised by Alice Waters of *Chez Panisse*. Aaron Copland once composed there, Ralph Ellison was the first black prize winner, and I could only wonder at what great works and learning would come from the genius of the current residents.

Our next stop in Rome, and the primary reason for the visit, was the Vatican Museum. We'd been invited to a press conference for a new book offering a different perspective on the iconography and meaning of Michelangelo's work in the Sistine Chapel. The invitation promised a *round table* discussion followed by a private visit to the Chapel, an experience I'd had the exquisite pleasure of once before, and was very excited about having the chance to repeat.

The *round table* discussion amounted to one long and tortuous speech after another, mostly from the publishers promoting the book. Then a scholar, no doubt very learned, went into an intricate and very difficult to follow (also for the Italians, I was later to discover) discourse on the assertions that the book put forward. Someone explained to me that the writer seemed to be saying that Michelangelo was showing, in his scenes from the Old Testament, predictions of New Testament events. It all seemed a bit far-fetched to me and certainly a difficult thing to prove. I'd hoped there'd be some debate, but no.

The talk took place in one of the many lavish and ornate rooms inside the Vatican Museum, close to the Sistine Chapel itself. As it approached 6.00pm there was a faint rumbling of thunder and looking up we could see the lightning through the huge glass dome in the center of the ceiling. The noise got louder. I leaned over to whisper to Alex,

This is God grumbling: forget all this analysis and symbolism, isn't it enough that Michelangelo's work is a masterpiece of beauty? Just shut up already, and let the people visit the Chapel.

A few days after the Rome visit, it was All Saints' Day, November 1st, an Italian national holiday. Whenever I had a free day I liked to hop on a train to some place in Italy I'd yet to visit. Along with some friends visiting from the US, I headed for Ferrara, about 50km northeast of Bologna in northern Italy. The town is listed as a UNESCO World Heritage Site and its beautiful wide streets and palazzos date from the 14th and 15th centuries. It was a glorious, crisp day and after lunch we wandered around with the thousands of Italians also taking their *passeggiata*. We didn't notice any other tourists or obvious ex-pats, so felt a part of the local scene, enjoying our holiday just like the Italians around us.

At the end of the day, we returned to the train station to be met with the surprising sight of over a 100 police in SWAT gear: billy clubs, helmets and shields. I asked one of them what was happening and he told me a soccer game had just finished. It seemed a bit excessive but I figured they were guarding the track to allow the opposing team to get on the Bologna train. We were waiting on the next track and got into position to take pictures of the celebrities (if only we'd known them from Adam). We were a bit puzzled when the police warned us not to take any photos. Then we discovered the police were there, not for the *players,* but to protect the *supporters.* I was very confused, but one of the policemen explained these were the fans from the opposing team, which had lost, and that they were very *arrabiatissimi* - angry. To prevent any violence it was necessary to guard them, to keep them separate from local fans when getting to and from the station, at the game, and on the train. We watched the fans arrive and board the specially allocated carriages.

As the train pulled out of the station, the SWAT team took off its helmets and shields and I guess went home to spend the rest of the holiday with family. The event left quite an impression on me. It was such a contrast to my experience of attending sporting events in the US. I was taken aback that such measures were actually necessary. I later shared my amazement at this event with a UK born friend who lived in England in the 80's and 90's. She gave me the same kind of withering look Marco gave me when I was excited at *discovering* what for him was *old news*.

The next day, it was back to work. I did an interview about *The Florentine* on a local Italian TV station for its 7.00pm news program. I'd had quite a bit of media experience when my books were published so it wasn't too big a deal for me, except for the no small matter of being interviewed in Italian. Still, it went well and I enjoyed the experience.

And so to the weekend and an invitation from an English friend, to a Guy Fawkes party at his villa on a hilltop near Lucca. There was a great crowd, over a 100 in all; multinational, multi-age and *molto* fun. The guests included Italians; British, including a big group of the host's 20 year-old son's friends; New Zealanders; and maybe two or three Americans besides me.

I stayed at nearby Villa Michaela, owned by my host's friends, who usually rent the place out to movie stars and the somewhat wealthier than I. It was fabulous - 13 bedrooms, each with enormous bathrooms, closets and views. Besides the three- storey main villa containing numerous sitting rooms, a piano room, libraries and a dining room with a table to sit 30, the estate included two swimming pools, and even a church! With an attention to detail and authenticity to the centuries-ago when it was built, each room was exquisitely furnished with gorgeous fabrics and adorned with striking paintings. Several of the other out of town party guests stayed there too. After the main events of the evening, the bonfire and food, we came back to the intimacy of the piano room, where we were treated to an impromptu concert of music and opera by the hosts and various guests, until 4.00am.

The next day we were invited to visit Villa Massei, home to Americans Paul Gervais and Gil Cohen since the early 80's. They took on the task of landscaping the villa's considerable gardens with stunning results; the story of the project became the subject of Paul's very successful book, *A Garden in Lucca*. The gardens are open to the public which can come to see how ancient, traditional and contemporary elements have been used to design one spectacular garden after another. I'd rate my own gardening knowledge, skills and experience on a similar level to those relating to my cooking expertise, but I took my cue from the British guests who clearly knew their plants and backyards and were all impressed by the detail, variety and combination. The end result, however, required no specialist insight to admire; it was easy to appreciate the beauty and serenity that had been created by this joyous meeting of nature's gifts with man's creativity and sheer hard work.

An Italian Prime Minister and gifted teacher; the American Academy; an exclusive visit to the Sistine Chapel; a SWAT team and an angry crowd of soccer supporters; a TV interview *in Italian; a* Guy Fawkes party and *A Garden in Lucca:* business as usual for the editor-in-chief of *The Florentine*. No nine to five for me.

One Giant Leap for Mankind

It was one of those moments in life, where I felt that maybe I was witnessing history in the making. I attended the dedication of Dynamo Camp, a member of Paul Newman's *Hole in the Wall Camps Association*. Newman started the first camp in Connecticut, over 20 years ago. He'd wanted to provide a place for children with chronic and life-threatening illnesses to have the chance to *raise a little hell* in the way that most kids like to do from time to time, all based upon the philosophy that fun and laughter are often the best medicines. The profits from *Newman's Own* products such as his popcorn, spaghetti sauces and salad dressings go to support these camps, now based worldwide, as well as to other charities. His recent death was a great sadness but his incredible legacy lives on through his inspired works of philanthropy.

When I first heard there was going to be a camp northwest of Florence at Pistoia, I knew that I had to get involved. Serena Porcari, the director of Dynamo came from Milan to meet me and my dynamic girlfriends. She met us for lunch at the Lungarno Hotel, as a guest of Louise Ferragamo. We told Serena, we were all in a position to have some influence when it came to raising awareness and funds. Besides Louise, we included a VP at General Electric, directors of US university campus' in Florence and me as the publisher of *The Florentine*. We thought we could help.

On her second visit to Florence, again lunching with us girls, Serena was greeted with an endorsement from *Ferragamo,* with Wanda Ferragamo now heading the group - and the news that we'd already raised €200,000.

Who are you women?

We're just friends, one of the group explained to Serena, *Nita got us together for dinners at her house, now we meet for lunch at our different fabulous offices, to laugh, gossip and make Louise take us shopping at Ferragamo. So we thought why not do something worthy together too?* Her response:

I want to go shopping at Ferragamo!

While the camp was still under construction, Serena arranged for us, now called *The Florence Committee,* to visit the Dynamo Camp which is located within a World Wildlife Foundation reserve. She wanted us to actually see what we were already enthusiastically supporting, as well as having us meet Enzo Manes, the businessman and philanthropist heading up the project. Though far from finished, it was already easy to see how the place was going to provide an extraordinary environment for the kids who would get to stay there, for free, to enjoy an extensive range of indoor and outdoor activities.

One of the more interesting challenges for the camp was actually finding the children to attend, though not because there weren't enough kids with the kind of illnesses that would make them eligible or that wouldn't have loved the experience. In the US, going to summer camp is a common activity for kids from all types of backgrounds, from Boy Scout and church camps, to rather more expensive variations of the same. In Italy, however, I met few people that even understood the word as a noun, as in *a camp.* Sure they knew about *camping* (though not many have experienced it). The concept of a place where kids went to stay and sleep, away from home and without their parents, even for short periods of time was very alien to them (also true when the 'kids' were adults!). And of course, in this instance, we are talking about kids who are very ill. The thought of sending a sick child away from his *Mama* was a hard sell.

We laughed when we toured the camp; it more closely resembled a 5-star mountain resort than anything I'd attended during my childhood summers - so Italian! The beautiful buildings, exquisite gardens, tasteful linens and scrumptious food were complimented by the very latest medical equipment and facilities. The idea was that the parents would be able to have complete confidence that their precious children would receive the best care and attention for the duration of their visit.

I knew that the event to celebrate the camp opening would be a perfect subject for a *Florentine* article. From the inception of the newspaper, I'd wanted to take advantage of our ability to reach a large audience. I was committed to extending the *making a difference* philosophy beyond improving the English speaking community's experience of Florence, to actually *doing good* in Italy by covering, and in doing so supporting, the efforts of not-for-profits and charities. Saying that, while there certainly are a number of organizations doing great works in Florence, services for those vulnerable and in need were not as obvious as in many countries, and were mainly church or state run. They were hard to uncover, but when we did, we did our best to help promote their work.

Knowing the readership of The Florentine, I was certain that the Dynamo Camp would be seen by them as both an understandable and credible endeavor. Many of the readers are American and I'm very proud of the culture of giving to those in need that my compatriots repeatedly demonstrate. In addition, which American hasn't heard of the great Paul Newman? Besides his acting, his philanthropic projects were widely recognized and his charitable works came with a well-deserved reputation for being well run. The Dynamo Camp was of course for Italian children - what better way for the ex-pats to feel they were making a contribution to the local community of which they were so pleased to be a part? At the same time, they could be confident that donations would be well spent and truly make a difference to those most in need. In addition, as the camp was registered as a US charity, anyone making donations would be able to take advantage of the tax benefits.

Each of the *Hole in the Wall Camps* is supported by an individual or group of philanthropists who are part of the association and responsible for coming up with the funds to buy and run the camp. At the Dynamo Camp, Enzo Manes, an Italian businessman was the key player and, on our first visit, an Italian girlfriend was clearly puzzled,

So *what's with Enzo? Who is he exactly?*

She didn't understand *why* he'd taken on this venture. She wanted to know why he'd be involved if he wasn't making money from his substantial investment.

I explained what to me was obvious. He was a successful businessman, and that like many others who have made a great deal of money, he came to a realisation that he had more than enough to finance his personal needs and those of his family. He wanted to use his wealth to help others. She found this strange, explaining to me, that within her 500 year-old family, the purpose of wealth was to provide for children and grandchildren *and* to support the next generations for another half millennium to come. Given that there could never be enough money to secure this extended future, the concept of having cash to give away was difficult for her to comprehend.

During my time in Italy I had many discussions with both Italians and ex-pats about the reasons Italians *don't give* in a way that is similar to that of Americans and many other nationalities. They've helped me to come to a number of conclusions. Primarily, Italians come from a culture where welfare or social services are presumably taken care of by the church and state, and since they already give to the church and pay taxes why should they offer any more? Also, there's a great, and justified, cynicism that if they do give money to an organization, corruption will prevent the money from being used to benefit those for whom it was intended. In addition, as there's little or no tax benefit to individuals who give money to non-profits, there's no extra incentive on that count either. This is in no way meant to imply that Italians are not extremely generous people. I've personally witnessed many exceptional acts of kindness to family, friends and employees that have involved emotional support as well as financial aid. It's just that the culture of giving to wider philanthropic ventures is traditionally much more limited.

Enzo Manes gave a speech at the opening of the Dynamo Camp that, I believe, went a long way to opening up a change in the hearts and minds of the 500 plus gathered around him. He started his speech, in Italian, of course, with the words,

Is it worth it?

He went on to describe his personal journey from the initial decision to *invest* in a non-profit, to his choice of what that venture would be, and then to his involvement in building the camp, staffing it, and finding the children who would attend. He answered his own question with conviction,

Yes, it is worth it.

After his speech, I spoke with many Italians, who came to the event, given their prominent political, social or business roles, out of duty. They shared that his speech had prompted them to question themselves about how they could give, and how they could use their wealth to make a real difference to those who most needed help. They agreed with me that something momentous had happened that Sunday...*one small step*...

Belonging

Weekends in Florence were a challenge for me especially after Tony and Montana had returned to LA. Busy from morning to night every day during the week, in a blink of an eye, it would be Saturday. I'd wake with nothing planned; no events to attend, no one with which to catch up for a quick caffé, no one to meet or interview. I would be plunged into hours of loneliness. I have no problem being alone in my apartment in LA with no weekend arrangements lined up; I live on the beach after all. But in Florence, Friday night would find me already looking forward to Monday.

The main challenge was that the Italians are so *in the moment* that they rarely plan or discuss their plans until events, including the weekend, are upon them. At the same time, ironically, when it comes to weekends and holidays, it's often the traditions of the past that determine where they are spent. Examples of this include: visiting relatives in the country *every* weekend; going to their *usual* village or town or place *by il mare* to spend the month of August; heading out to the *same* ski venue for *settimana Bianca* - the *white week*. In addition, the expression *Natale da noi, La Pasqua da voi*, meaning *Christmas with us* (family), *Easter on your own* (usually with friends), dictates how this Catholic nation will spend its most important holidays.

A few days before one of my Easters in Florence, I was having un caffé with a few friends who started talking about

239

where they were heading off to spend the holiday. Having no plans of my own, I felt left out and sorry for myself. Betta was telling us about the many people who'd be joining her, and her husband Francesco, at their home in Maremma. She explained who'd be arriving with whom and it sounded like quite a gathering. Time, I decided, for one of those *pushy Nita requests* and so the, by this point, needy Americana pipes up,

Would there be room for me?

Betta's surprise wasn't at my nerve, as I've discovered on other occasions, but at the fact that I actually would *like* to join them.

Ti piacerebbe venire? You'd like to come?

It would never occur to an Italian that someone wouldn't have a pre-ordained place to be at such a holiday. She was happy for me to come and I was very relieved to have a place to go and knew that my *chutzpah* had successfully headed off a gloomy few days.

Friday afternoon and I was on the way to Betta's *casa colonica*, her family's country home. Its ten en-suite bedrooms come complete with the crispest fine linens and the fluffiest towels. The kitchen is impressive enough to wow even this abstemious cook. The huge dining room is notable, not least of all, because of the caffé, tea and pastries it makes available throughout the day. Need I add that there's also a swimming pool, tennis courts and extensive gardens? And dogs? And horses? But while all very enjoyable, experiencing this luxury didn't turn out to be the *most* impressive thing about my weekend with Betta and Francesco.

All the property and land surrounding my friends' country home belongs to Betta's family and has done for generations. We stopped by to visit her parents' home and had dinner at the cousins who, while they lived in Rome, were up at *their place* for the weekend. On Saturday afternoon, everyone went to the beach to play, relax and see friends from Milan, who would also come over for drinks that evening. We came and went, as did many others; arrangements were fluid, great food and wine just appeared. We took a bike ride, stopped off to buy a particular kind of cheese; each moment seemed special in a different way.

Sunday morning arrived and in our country casual clothes, we headed to the beautiful, medieval church in the village for Easter services. It was packed. The setting was quaint, charming and yet the parishioners were far from old-fashioned; generations of families were out in force, dressed in country cashmeres and leathers, not a pastel suit or bonnet among them!

I was the only non-Italian. By what great fortune did I get to be here? Why am I sitting in a Catholic church, three hours outside Florence, in a village with a name I don't even know? How, is it that, although I have only visited Betta here once before, I know almost half the people around me?

After church, in a caravan of five cars, our group drove to another village to a medieval castle at the top of a mountain, the *second* home of friends of Betta and Francesco. Carlo and his wife have their main residence in Siena and are in the wine business. They'd recently bought the castle, which they had completely renovated. They'd also purchased its surrounding vineyards. It was like a museum, replete with cannons and chainmail armor (alas no moat) in the courtyard, all providing hours of fun and re-enactment opportunities for the kids.

The dining room where we ate our Easter meal had 4 round tables and sat maybe 30 guests in all. The host sat at one table, the hostess at another, later switching tables. Waiters served us with beautiful wine, the best prosciutto, a selection of cheese and a risotto followed by several roasted meats. It was all very formal. I thanked God for my Italian, because again, I was the only American, and was thrilled to be able to hold my own in the fascinating and high brow conversations that flowed between the guests: journalists from Rome, writers from Milan, vintners from Siena.

As the meal progressed, I couldn't help commenting to Francesco who, like his wife, comes from an old noble family, that Carlo's formal demeanor and Count-like dress were, well, a *bit pretentious*. I asked,

Is he from a noble family? Francesco laughed,

Of course not, why else would he buy this monstrosity and act this way?

Later in the afternoon, another cousin hosted an Easter egg hunt and put on a fabulous spread of food. The kids, eggs all found, played soccer, rode bikes to and from the different family homes and paddled in the pond. It was a lovely relaxed ending to a very packed weekend.

As I had an appointment in Florence the next day, I traveled home that evening by myself, contemplating the mix of emotions my full-to-the-brim weekend had stirred up in me. I had been embraced by this extended family with its many generations and wide spread of siblings and cousins. Everyone's generous nature had made me feel *one of them*, I was able to be myself, be *at home*, an experience greatly helped by the fact that I could so easily communicate with them in Italian. I got to intimately experience family life in Italy: *belonging*.

The bitter to the sweetness of the joy and warmth I felt, was my knowing that this was the same intensity of emotion and connection I had always wanted to feel within my own family...to have grandparents, parents, uncles, aunts, cousins, all gathered together in one place, celebrating important occasions together. I knew, for me, that this could never be. I'd left Detroit when quite young, as had others in our extended family. Contact with aunts, uncles and cousins had dropped away, many of the older generations, including my parents and all of my grandparents, had passed on.

As a child, our family never had a summer or country cottage to which we could always go back, where the wider family could spend holidays, or a place where we could bring our friends, boyfriends, husbands and children to gather for weekends and celebrations. When I had children myself, I kept opting for spending money on family travel rather than a permanent home or vacation cabin. I don't regret this choice; I just wish that we had had enough money to do both. Now that my children are older, I realize they too have no place, other than their own houses, to call home. Reflecting on my recent weekend, it was strange to find that such profound sadness could sit alongside the feelings of incredible joy gifted by my few days away.

Several months later, I was in synagogue in LA. Usually, I sit with my girlfriends but this time I was there alone. At one part of the Saturday service, the congregation sings a very lively song and the children, excited, rush up to the *bima* to open the ark and take out the Torah. As is always the case, I find myself crying. My tears come when I see the joy of the kids (in contrast to my own childhood's very restrained and formal experience of the synagogue) and this reminds me I am here by myself, without my family (Tony and the kids only rarely join me and what is left of my extended family is geographically distanced). I look over at one of the regulars, David, who noticed my tears and I explain,

I cry at this part, because it's such a joyous family ritual and I don't have family with me. He looked puzzled,

Nita, this is your family!

I'm forever impressed by Italian friends who know their ancestry back to the 1500s and at how many of them still live in the same city, village, or even palazzo, as the past generations of their family. However, in the moment that David responded as he did, I realized that I can trace my family much further back, to over 5700 years ago. I reflected that during my life, I have attended synagogue in many places including Bucharest, Leningrad, Prague and Italy. And each time, I have felt very much *at home* with those around me, chanting the same prayers, singing the same songs, praising the same God and, even reading the Hebrew from the prayer book.

So I do have *a place*, somewhere I can always go and where I can talk and listen and laugh - and cry - with generations to whom I have a long and close connection. It's not a palazzo, or a castle, or a coastal retreat; it's a *shul*. No matter where in the world I am, it will always be a weekend home, a place to catch up with the family; a place where I belong.

When Push Comes to Shove

Fashion shows in Italy are all about making a stunning impact and outdoing the competition in terms of the *wow factor* and media coverage. I'd often see this in action during *Pitti Uomo,* men's fashion week, which takes place in Florence twice a year. Buyers from all over the world come to view and place orders for men's clothing for the following season. Each week of fashion frenzy involves catwalk shows, art exhibits, parties, celebrity appearances and a few surprises created to steal the limelight from the competition.

Invites arrived in our office to attend numerous parties surrounding *Pitti Uomo.* I loved these events, but it was always the related fashion or art itself I found entertaining; any actual *party* I'd find pretty unsatisfactory. I certainly had no attachment, unlike many of the guests, to the bizarre concept of *being seen.* Invariably, the same crowd would appear, dressed much more conservatively than their *fashionista* counterparts in Milan, where they are always more courageous, sophisticated and unique in their way of dressing. In Florence it's all black, nothing you'd see as *cutting-edge* and, of course, nothing without a label: *Gucci, Valentino, Prada,* etc. Milan, of course, also likes its labels but there it's more important to be up-to-date on the latest, breakthrough designers as well.

Even if there are new, interesting or important people I'd want to meet at these events, the music is so loud that conversation is impossible. Yet, despite the dominance of the music, there's very little dancing which would at least partly compensate for the lack of opportunity to talk and meet new people. Mostly, it's just little cliques, standing around looking and commenting on the other little cliques standing around and doing the same thing. I love fashion and while it's certainly not why I moved to Florence, I did think the fashion scene would have a little more of an *edge* to it - it's one of the few things about the great city that didn't meet my expectations. Except that is, for one event...

It was the June *Pitti Uomo* in 2006 and Roberto Cavalli, the brilliant and notorious Florentine designer (he was convicted of tax evasion - in the US he would have been in jail for years, somehow it works differently in Italy) had pulled whatever strings were necessary to orchestrate a fashion show on one of Florence's great icons, the Ponte Vecchio, home for 500 years to its famous jewelers and goldsmiths. The combination of the venue and Cavalli's bold and innovative talent provided a 100% guarantee that the event was going to be spectacular. Imagine standing on the closed-off bridge, sipping an *aperitivo* and looking out onto the floodlit Uffizi Gallery, the Arno gently flowing below, the historic palazzos standing proud along its banks - and a creative parade of color and imagination about to unfold before you. Even the most jaded and over-worked fashion model would surely perk up at the experience of having the Ponte Vecchio for a catwalk?

Several months before, we'd gotten wind of this once in a lifetime occasion at *The Florentine*. I told Marco that we *had to be* there and asked if he could call the designer's press office to get an invite. He obliged and was promised we'd be put on the list. I assumed it was handled and when, the week before we still had no invite, I had Marco call again only for him to be told there was no room for us. We continually struggled with the fact that because Italians didn't read *The Florentine*, we were usually on the bottom of the list (if on the list at all!) of the must-attend press for popular events. I called the *Cavalli* press office myself, dozens of times - no answer. I left endless voicemails. Finally, I spoke with a real person only to be told, she was sorry but she simply couldn't get us an invite. I begged. I pleaded. I begged again; all to no avail.

The day of the event arrived. I was distraught. I bumped into friends on the way to get their hair done or to pick up their dresses from dry-cleaning, all for the big show. I was jealous, defeated; it was ugly. I'd tried everything to get an invite. Even the friend with whom I shared my apartment, whose fiancé was in the fashion industry, couldn't help,

Sorry, she offered, sheepishly, also explaining that not only was she going to the fashion show with her man, but that after the event,

We're popping over to Cavalli's house for dinner. Just great!

Cycling home from the office, over what had now become the offending *old bridge*, I was feeling extremely sorry for myself. As I got near my apartment, I spotted a Government Minister who I'd interviewed many months earlier. I stopped to say hello and, as social convention demands the world over, he inquired politely as to my welfare. My answer visibly took him aback,

I'm so depressed! Probably anxious to get home having just escaped the office, he had little choice but to ask me why. I told him how desperately I wanted to attend the *Cavalli* fashion show, about to start in not much more than an hour, but that I ridiculously found myself without an invite. He was straight on the phone and asking favors - for me! He called one guy, and I could barely follow the quick, colloquial Italian, but I did catch,

You know - it's me, your Communist friend.

I love Florence! The man had indeed once been in the Communist Party and it was, in Italy, hardly a shocking thing to say, even to his most likely conservative contact in the fashion industry, but still, to an American...

Unfortunately, after such kindness, the Minister struck out too. I went home to continue to sulk; but I couldn't keep up so much misery without taking action for long. I changed into a simple black wrap dress, got back on my bike and decided to give the old *chutzpah* a bit of a work out. My plan, as far as I had one, was to pretend I was on the list, show my business card and talk my way in. I had nothing to lose.

I arrived at the Ponte Vecchio. Doing my best to *act casual,* I joined the line to give my name to one of the several PR women guarding their source of power: *The List of Invitees.* I waited as they either allowed people through or told them, firmly, that as their names were not on the list they would, regrettably, be unable to enter. I was nearing the front of the pack, racking my brains for something clever to say that would get me over the line where others had failed, when in a moment of exquisite timing, (the PR bulldogs' eyes down on their clipboards) an angel (whose anonymity I will preserve until death) reached out and grabbed my hand, pulling me from the purgatory of limbo on the *outside* and all but shoving me into the heavenly throng *inside.*

And there I was with a glass of sparkling in hand, chatting with my friends and nosing into my signature leopard print *Cavalli* gift bag.

After some minutes socializing, we were requested to take our seats lining the bridge. The street lights went off and the runway lights came on - cue Naomi Campbell strutting down the Ponte Vecchio in a stunning emerald green *Cavalli* dress. It was breathtaking - amazed silence and then rapturous applause. Famous Italian personalities came next, including a soap-opera star and television journalist, and we continued to feast on many more gorgeous designs. Before long, Naomi was back in another knockout gown, this time in white. And lastly, the man himself, Roberto Cavalli, strolling across the iconic bridge to a standing ovation,

Bravo! Bravissimo!

I was elated that my persistence had paid off and that, after all the drama involved in getting in, the event had actually exceeded my expectations. Could the evening get any better? Yes! My roommate's fiancé *insisted* I go with them to Roberto Cavalli's for dinner and, after a 30-minute journey to the outskirts of Florence, we passed the enormous horse sculptures *(Cavalli* is Italian for horses) and drove up to the designer's majestic home. I drank in every detail: more sculptures, striking pieces of furniture and art, animal print fabrics, all screaming out with the distinctive style of the hugely talented owner.

The dinner was held in the garden, dramatically lit tables overflowed with seafood and *Cavalli* designed plates, linens and cutlery, catering for the many guests. At one point during the leisurely meal I spoke with Leonardo Ferragamo, uncle to Jamie. Leonardo had lived his entire life in Florence and was himself a major figure in the fashion industry. He described the Ponte Vecchio event as the most extraordinary sight he'd seen in his life.

Dinner over, I danced until the small hours.

Two weeks later, I was back in LA and Marco sent me a photo, printed on the front page of an Italian newspaper the day after that magical evening. The picture shows Ms. Campbell strutting across the Ponte Vecchio. The only other in-focus face in the photo, sitting in the front row, a huge smile saying it all, was that of... *La Nita.*

No Laughing Matter

Arriving at the local television studio, Linda Falcone, *The Florentine* managing editor and I found ourselves the only Americans on a panel of women discussing *violenza - rape*. In Italy, this is not a frequent topic of discussion among women, journalists or the wider public. Because of this you would have thought that there wasn't much incidence of it; or be led to wonder if it did happen and just wasn't covered in the news; or believe that it maybe wasn't even reported to the police in the first place. However, Linda and I knew personally from our contacts with the US universities and the US Consulate that there was actually a frightening amount of incidents of rape in Italy, with American college students being frequent victims.

Not to excuse the perpetrators in any way whatsoever, one dean of students explained to me that 99% of incidents of crime against Americans in Florence involved the victims being under the influence of excessive alcohol. She explained,

The plain truth is that when people are drunk, their reactions will not be quick or smart; and their decisions will be poor. Young and drunk female college students, stumbling home along unlit streets in the early hours of the morning prove all too vulnerable to muggings and rape.

The US Consul General and embassy, liaising with the Italian authorities and the universities were aggressively working to reduce, if not completely eliminate, the number of incidences of rape. The universities held talks for the students, bringing in the infamous police chief, known for his no nonsense tactics. In addition, the city authorities made agreements with the taxi companies to pay for rides for women after a certain hour in the evening, and the pubs and bars were asked to be responsible for no longer serving drinks to those who were already *ubriaci*. The effort was well co-ordinated.

The week before the television program was aired, Nora Dempsey, the US Consul General, had issued a warning to women students not to walk alone in the streets of Florence in the dark, especially after midnight. Her comments sparked off the considerable controversy which had led to the theme of the program and our invitation to participate. Covered extensively on TV news programs and radio bulletins, and in the editorial sections of the Italian newspapers, there were headlines such as: *American Consul General says Florence is unsafe!* And, *US students are not safe in Florence!* And, *Consul General says women need to move in packs to ward off Florentine crime!*

The Florentines felt attacked, accused, unfairly judged and extremely insulted; this was the mood Linda and I walked into as the representative Americans at the TV studio. The usual male and female hosts of the weekly, issue-oriented program were going to moderate the discussion. The main panel consisted of Italian women and Linda who is Italian-American. I was part of another group seated on bleachers just to the side, but still on camera, who could also participate in the discussion. Linda sat alongside a psychiatrist; a social worker; a woman who was the director of an agency which helped abused and battered women; a lawyer; and a woman who held a position with Human Services for the *Comune*.

Casting my eyes across this panel of distinguished women I was taken aback to see they were all dressed as if for a cocktail party: big hair; layers of make-up; diamonds galore - multiple-strand bracelets sending blinding shards of light in all directions; and cleavage, lots of it. I don't know quite why I was so shocked, maybe just the sight of them all together. I'd certainly seen this before in Italy, professional women of all ages including doctors, lawyers, bankers, engineers, professors; many of them fighting to be taken more seriously alongside their male colleagues, while simultaneously aspiring to the seductive 'call-girl' look. Linda and I were dressed in what we thought was appropriate to the subject, simple black suits. *We* looked out of place!

Most of the program was devoted to the challenging topic of rape in Italy, not specifically Nora's comments. Statistics were given, including estimates of how much rape was likely to go unreported. The reasons why non-reporting was so prevalent were discussed, the most significant being that a family member was the rapist. How the crimes and criminals were subsequently dealt with under the law, was also explored.

Given that the conversation was in Italian, *rapid* Italian, with a lot of back and forth, at times it was difficult for me to follow, but I got the essence. One of the things that I found fascinating was the discussion around how girls and women should be free to dress however they want. Now I totally agree with this, but if the reality was that somehow *seductive dress* increased the chances of attack (it's certainly never the *cause* of attack), then I was surprised that these mothers were so vehemently against encouraging their daughters to consider what they wore and to think about covering up when out on the street late at night.

The other thing that I couldn't help notice, and felt uncomfortable about, was how *smiley* and light-hearted everyone seemed to be. The whole tone of things seemed out of step with the seriousness of the topic. When, for example, Linda was asked about Nora's statement, she explained how in some US universities, when a woman student had to stay on campus late in the evening to study or work in a lab, she could call upon the campus police to escort her back to her dorm. The audience actually laughed! I was astounded. The male host made a comment about how hypocritical Americans were, claiming to be the *land of the free* and yet, operating like a police state. This was followed by a lambasting of Nora Dempsey's comments regarding the safety of young women in Florence, seen as totally unjustified in light of the horrendous crime rates in places like New York, with a special mention for Beverly Hills.

This tipped me over the edge and seeing my obvious exasperation as the likely source of some entertaining controversy, a microphone was thrust into my face. My Italian was far from accurate, but I have never had problems expressing myself in any language! I said,

First of all: I think this is a very, very serious topic, and I can't understand all the smiling and joking going on. *I live in Florence with my daughter. We also spend a lot of time in Beverly Hills* (close enough anyway). *I don't want my daughter walking around either place alone at night. I would never consider the police escort mentioned a restriction on my freedom, but a show of concern for my safety. Of course we should be able to wear whatever we want, but that's kind of a moot point after you've been raped. And as far as Nora being accused of wrongfully labeling Florence as unsafe, which she never actually said, I ask how many of you lock the doors of your homes or automobiles? All of you do. Not because Florence is an unsafe place, but because you are smart, and you want to do what you can to protect yourself against those unsafe elements that do exist within it. This is what Nora is advising the students to do, to be* smart and do what they can to prevent becoming victims of crime.

Even in my horrid Italian, I knew my point had made an impact, the mood changed and the program moved in a more serious and constructive direction. On the way home, Linda and I were questioning how the earlier light-hearted-ness had been possible.

I thought about it and said to Linda,

I bet that none of them have been raped or have ever even known anyone that had been the victim of a rape or other sexual attack. You can't have experienced such trauma - or known someone who has (as Linda and I did) - *and talk so lightly about it. Anything other than a mood of gravity would have been impossible.*

Giacomo, Marco's brother, who also works on *The Florentine*, and who had accompanied us to the filming, said to the guys back at the office,

Nita was the only one who said what really needed to be said on the program. And the others listened. We all need to listen.

It was satisfying to hear my communication was received in this way but, I would be much more rewarded if I thought that my words could, in any way, have helped to prevent even one attack.

Pillow Flight

To celebrate the 80 years since Salvatore Ferragamo founded the company that his heirs have so successfully continued and expanded, the family decided to publish a children's book with proceeds from sales going to a children's charity. The characters in the story book were created from the animal prints found on many of the *Ferragamo* scarves. For the book's launch, a party was given for the children and grandchildren of many of Florence's influential families, including the siblings and cousins of the Ferragamo clan, who were invited to the country estate, Il Borro.

The event was held late in the afternoon on a weekday, so it was noticeable how few men were around, work commitments keeping them from their families. My own invite, as I had no children to bring along, was in my member-of-the-press capacity. Driving up the elegant, tree-lined road to the main villa, passing the polo fields and some of the many vineyards, it was an extraordinary sight to see, floating above the poplar trees, a huge hot-air balloon made from classic *Ferragamo* animal-prints.

The road opened up into gardens hosting many children's attractions: trampolines, clowns, games and, not surprisingly, hot-air balloon rides. The adults were dressed in city rather than country attire, the kids in school uniforms; the mix of formality and fun, along with the outside venue and hot sun, made me think of a long ago royal garden party at Versailles.

Tables were laden with food. The fare at children's parties in Italy has little connection with the fat and sugar filled delights served at their American equivalent. Admittedly, I have moments when I crave such junk. When invited to a Halloween party in Florence, a holiday not traditionally celebrated in Italy, I'd been disappointed not to get my hands on some candy corn or a *Snickers* bar at the very least. Instead, in the huge banquet *sala* of the grand palazzo where the party was held, I'd been met with tables filled with *aperitivos* of fine cheese; prosciutto; a huge, roast prime beef; bruschettas of fresh tomatoes and pate. The nearest thing to what I'd been hoping for was the table of delicate pastries, but still a million miles away from what I had sugar-cravingly envisaged. The food was of a similarly sophisticated kind at this party, though I did find two fast-food treats: a table serving pizza and one where ice cream sundaes were being made to order, albeit with artisan gelato.

There were lovely, intimate seating areas throughout the garden. The outdoor furniture was elegantly appointed with silk pillows made of the *Ferragamo* animal-prints used in the storybook and for the hot-air balloon (the same patchwork design would be the key fabric in the new spring line of *Ferragamo* purses). These pillows were stunning!

From the time we arrived, my friend, who will not be named, but who is a very well-known and respected member of the ex-pat community in Florence, demanded of me,

How do we get one of those pillows? Then, at regular intervals throughout the afternoon she would whisper the likes of:

Do you think they would miss one if I stuck it under my jacket? These pillows would look perfect on my living room sofa. Nita, just grab one, no one will notice!

Her desire to be in possession of one or more of these luscious objects became further heightened by seeing another friend leaving with a bag full of them, presumed to be a gift from Wanda Ferragamo. So, to satisfy her who must not be named, I went up to Jamie Ferragamo, my landlord, friend and party host and inquired as to who it was necessary to sleep with, in order to get one of the fabulous pillows. With a glint in his eye, Jamie told me to just take some. So we did. We were discreet. Well, as discreet as we could be given we were carrying three pillows each.

The next day, a friend of mine called. He'd also been at the party, and had driven there and back, in style, with one of the Ferragamos. The friend had neither asked for a pillow or been offered one, and though delighted at his limo ride, was envious of the loot we had acquired. However, he shared with us the pillow-related scandal that he'd discovered on a visit to the *Ferragamo* offices the day after the party. It turned out that the marketing department had *borrowed* the pillows from the *Ferragamo* store just for the event. Somewhat taken aback by the number that seemed to be missing, they were in uproar after being informed they were going to have foot the bill. Naturally I felt a bit guilty, but not guilty enough to confess, though I did at least make sure no one was *personally* going to have pay from his or her own pocket.

I sent off a hasty e-mail to my partner in crime, telling her what had happened. Her reply was straightforward enough,
What pillows?

From then on, whenever I visit Jamie and Louise, upon my departure, Jamie shouts out to Louise,
Hey, check Nita's bags for stolen goods!

I Went There Tomorrow

Nita's salons, along with my week-before-US-Thanksgiving dinners, were traditions I cultivated while in Florence, inviting friends and associates to my home for an *aperitivo*, seeking to bring together the fascinating people that I'd come to meet in my social and working life. I loved being able to make new introductions and help build connections especially between women who may not otherwise have come across each other in the normal course of their lives. Many of these friendships have lasted way beyond my time living in Florence.

I guess my guests found it a little alarming at first, but soon got more comfortable with my custom of halting the conversation and drinks and eats mid-flow, to call upon each of them to share something about their lives. It would often be along the lines of,

What are you passionate about in your life at this time?
What do you feel most grateful for right now?

I was once taught that you never should call on Italians to speak one at a time; not only are they more used to speaking all at once, but when put on the spot they will go silent, be uncomfortable. A frequent response to my invitations was,

I'm not coming if you are going to make me talk!

But people did accept regardless, and knew in particular when they sat around the table at Thanksgiving they *would* be called upon, each in turn, to give thanks. And I think, exactly because it is not their usual custom, that these occasions were even more memorable and moving for them. I'm proud to be known for bringing out their inspiring and intimate insights and the conversations that resulted from such sharing.

When I planned Thanksgiving, or any of my more regular get-togethers, I'd typically send out an invite via e-mail three weeks in advance. This worked quite well with my expat circle but, I soon realized, was a totally ineffective way to secure the attendance of my Italian friends. It wouldn't matter that I gave the specific date, day of the week, time, month, year and current astrological alignment, the Italians would think I was inviting them for *the week in which I sent the invitation*. I'd even have people ringing my doorbell that very same week. It took me a while to work it out, but it finally dawned on me that this phenomenon was connected to the Italian perspective on all things *future*.

Through my work as a management consultant I've spent a lot of time looking at how language shapes our thoughts, actions and experiences and how our choice of words impacts how the world shows up for us. When a leader tells me, that they'll *try* to do something, I don't expect action; when they announce that they *commit* to an action or goal, I look forward to seeing it happen and great results coming from it. I believe *it's all semantics* - rather than *it's just semantics*.

It was my fascination with how language shapes action that got me thinking about the relationship between the 14 or so *everyday tenses* (there are others) that are used, in Italian, to describe the *past*. There's a tense which is used for describing the general past and one to denote things that usually happen. There's another tense that describes something that has happened and is completely over and done. Another tense, *passato remoto*, talks about a long time ago, think the Renaissance as opposed to your last trip to the beauty salon. There are also tenses for talking about the past in a literary way, or a journalistic way. The rules and conventions which guide the choice of the right past tense are an example of one of the things that make Italian such an intricate and beautiful language. This is also no coincidence. When you think of Italy, it is a country that has a remarkable and rich past; of course it would need 14 tenses to adequately explain and explore it. Mostly among young Italians, a much heard complaint is that Italy is *stuck in the past*. I can't tell you how many times, I've heard talented, but unappreciated contemporary Italian artists grumble at Florence's status as the city of European rebirth - pointing out that the *Renaissance* was, in fact, 500 years ago!

Maybe it's the relative predominance of *past* tenses - and the contrastingly limited amount of language available to talk about the *future* - that gives rise to my Italian girlfriends' challenge in looking ahead beyond a week. Yes, there are a few tenses that describe what is yet to happen, but really only one is commonly used and even that is regularly passed over in favor of a present tense employed to express the same meaning. *Lavo la biancheria,* meaning *I wash the sheets,* will equally be used to explain *I am washing the sheets right now* - as it will be for *I am washing the sheets the next day, week or month*.

I overheard another charming example of a linguistic challenge with the future, when walking along the street in Florence one day. A young Italian boy, talking in English to the American girl alongside him, replied to her question about his plans to visit somewhere or other,

Oh, I went there tomorrow.

I guess lifestyle in the US seems much more future-focused: the next steps; the drive to innovate; the forecast;

the go-forward plan for the month, the quarter, the year; the five year strategy. There doesn't seem to be a lot of time for the *now*. Self-improvement gurus, psychological experts and teachers of religion and philosophy urge us to stop for a moment in order to experience and appreciate the present. As well as seeking to perpetually propel ourselves beyond the now and into the new and unknown, Americans are often ridiculed as a nation for their ignorance of the past and their own nation's history, both the facts of it and the lessons that may be learned from reflecting upon it. Maybe we need a few more tenses to help us better connect with the present, and some more again, to encourage us to do some looking back.

So, yes, as to the future, I personally look ahead a lot too, but I'm far from a compulsive planner, unlike a number of my US friends. I'll often think about my *next* trip, whether to Italy, or for work, or maybe to visit my family. I'll scan the calendar for possible time slots, looking to squeeze things in around book club meetings, social events or other commitments. Italians, in my experience, do much less of this planning. An Italian friend was consulting me about a fundraising project. As part of the event, those involved were going to create, and then sell, a calendar. It was October at the time so I advised,

Stefano, you have to schedule all the photo shoots for the calendar immediately, it may even be too late!

He laughed; he understood my panic, having worked a lot in the US. He reminded me,

Nita, I know you'd buy your next year calendars in September of the year before, but Italians won't usually get one until the January or February of the New Year, if at all.

It wasn't just getting my Italian friends to my evening get-togethers that made this lack of future focus a challenge for me - scheduling business meetings was also an endless exercise in frustration. I'd look at my calendar for the day ahead and see that I had five or six meetings booked and, even when I made a point of confirming them the day before, at least half of them wouldn't happen. I'd call to ask where someone was and learn that they were in Milan, or overseas, or in another meeting and they'd call when they got back. Got back? When? That evening? Tomorrow? Next week? I used to think it was something about *me* or *The Florentine* that explained the cancellations, but no, I learned that it was *just how things were.*

Even after years in Florence, it's been hard to adjust my thinking. An up-coming trip will still find me e-mailing my Italian friends to make plans a couple of months beforehand only to arrive with nothing confirmed and wondering how I'm going to fill the days ahead. But in the cab from the airport into town, I start making calls and people answer the phone. It's like I've never left Florence. I'm suddenly busy from the moment I drop off my bags at where I'm staying, until I leave ten days later.

I guess if you want to fully embrace *la dolce vita,* in Florence, or indeed anywhere in Italy, you need not only to speak the language, but let the language speak to you.

Stranger than Fiction

And I thought *I* got more than I bargained for when I headed off to Italy to fulfill my dream of living in Europe. Doug and Christine Preston, good friends of ours from when we lived in Santa Fe, who moved to Florence four years before us, may have just trumped me. Doug, a journalist and murder-mystery writer, had also held onto a long-time wish to live in Italy and, while on assignment in Florence for *The New Yorker* magazine, he'd rung Christine to ask her what she thought of the idea of living there. She loved the idea, and so in 2000, along with their children, they'd set up home in a small village outside of Florence in the countryside. Doug soon began plotting his next novel, set naturally enough in Florence. Little did our friends know that their lives would soon become entwined with the life, not of a character from Doug's literary imagination, but of a real-life killer: *The Monster of Florence.*

In search of information about Italian police procedure, Doug went to meet Mario Spezi, a well-known and long-time crime reporter for *La Nazione.* Early on in their discussion, Doug shared that he was living in Giogoli. Mario told him about a crime that had been committed close to Doug's new home, the horrific murder of a young couple making love in their car. Doug, his crime-writing instincts aroused, was to learn that this was just one of seven such double-homicides that had taken place, in similar circumstances, around the countryside of Florence between 1974 and 1985. It was Mario, as the journalist first called to the scene, who had labeled the unknown killer as *The Monster of Florence.* His extensive research, investigation and reporting on the murders and events surrounding them, also earned Mario his own title: *The Monstrologer.*

In this and many subsequent meetings with Mario, Doug was to learn the incredible, *if-someone-had-made-it-up-you-wouldn't-believe-it* story of, not just the murders themselves, but the massive, expensive, convoluted and mismanaged police investigation and legal process surrounding the mission to convict a killer for the heinous crimes. Doug was hooked, and soon he and Mario were in partnership, writing a book about the events surrounding the murders, including the false allegations, wrongful arrests, conspiracies and cover-ups. Neither had a clue, when embarking on this venture, the extent to which they were to become not only characters, but worse, victims, in the very story they were telling in their intriguing and riveting book, *Dolci Colline de Sangue...Sweet Hills of Blood.*

As it happened, Doug and Christine's four year stay ended two months before we arrived. We inherited much of their furniture, books, phone cords and bicycles, but their most treasured legacy was the introductions they'd made to their fascinating and kind friends. It was on one of Christine's trips back to visit that I first met Mario and his Belgian wife Myriam, when they came to our house to see her. The couple both spoke very little English, but that didn't stop Mario's mischievous, dry, humor being immediately apparent and, similarly, Myriam's gracious nature. I could see why Doug and Christine had become firm friends with them.

By the time I met Mario and Myriam, he and Doug had most of their book written, in Italian, and they were finishing it off via e-mails and phone calls. Mario, desperately in need of money (I was well aware by then of how hard it was to make money as a journalist!), was encouraging Doug to do an English language version of the book. Doug, for practical reasons, wanted to get a contract and advance from a publisher before investing the enormous time it would take to do a translation. He'd put out some feelers, but no one was nibbling. Doug had funding for other books in place, and could afford to let it ride, but he really wanted to get something happening for Mario's sake.

Much later, when I'd been living in Florence for two years, and still residing in my magnificent abode in Via Ghibellina, Doug let me know he was coming to Florence to work on some last pieces of research for the book. Since I was leaving for a visit to LA, he was able to have my place to himself for most of his intended stay, our comings and goings overlapping a few days at the beginning and end of his trip. Just before I headed off, I gave a dinner party for him, inviting Mario and Myriam and other mutual friends; we all spent a lovely evening together. I left for LA the next day.

When I returned to Italy, I was thrilled to see Christine staying in my place! When Doug realized he would have the whole of the stunning apartment to himself, he'd asked her to bring their kids and join him. So where was Doug? And why did Christine seem so distressed? In my absence, it seems, I'd missed an unfolding nightmare that had, by this point, led to Doug being informed by the police that it was in his best interests to leave Italy...and not come back.

He'd taken them seriously.

Doug had been walking back to the apartment on Via Ghibellina, after un caffè, when he received a call from a police detective wanting to question him. Doug didn't want to tell the police exactly where he was staying, so he met the man and a second detective at the Palazzo Vecchio. Doug was presented with a legal summons to appear before the public minister of Perugia, in Umbria, and so he headed there the next day.

Towards the end of a very difficult interrogation, Doug was accused of, among other things, planting evidence, or at least attempting to plant it, in a building in the grounds of a villa in the Tuscan countryside (he had indeed been in the grounds of a villa with Mario, a place open to the public - they had been following a lead and had kept well clear of the specific building in question). The reasoning attributed to their alleged actions was an attempt to deflect suspicion from Mario, who for some time, incredulously, had been under investigation in connection with the murder of a Perugian doctor. The dead man had been rumored, at one point, to have been *The Monster of Florence*. The original suicide verdict attached to his death had been overturned following an exhumation. It was all so unbelievable and not just for Mario. The last, thought-to-be-related murder had occurred more than 20 years before and it was hard to see how anyone could conceive that Doug, a fiction writer, would be involved in any kind of cover-up.

Doug was told in no uncertain terms to leave the country,

Make no mistake; we will imprison you for obstruction of justice.

He was angry as well as frightened.

I'm pretty tough, but these interrogators are trained to break the Mafia! I was shaking in my shoes!

He was even more concerned for Mario's welfare than his own. Mario was also afraid for himself, and as it turned out, he had every reason to be. He knew that things were heading towards him being accused of actually being *The Monster of Florence*. As I said, you couldn't write it, though of course, after the events they both did; I highly recommend the English translation of their book re-titled as simply: *The Monster of Florence*.

Given how ridiculous it all seemed, perhaps it shouldn't have been a surprise, but still was, when several weeks later

Mario was taken from his home. ANSA (the Italian news agency) and Reuters broke the story that he had been arrested for obstruction of justice. He was put in solitary confinement for five days with no access to his wife or attorney, conditions allowed only in the pursuit of high profile mafia criminals and terrorists and certainly not journalists! In total, he spent 23 days imprisoned. The appeals court would later deem that his arrest and retention were totally illegal.

For his family and friends on the outside, his incarceration was also a nightmare. Doug was doing as much as he could from the US, calling the State Department, the Embassy, human rights and journalistic organizations. He sent details of his story and pleas for help to every major newspaper and magazine. I wanted to help too, at least reach out to Myriam, but because they had originally tracked down Doug from taps on Mario's phones, Doug advised me not to call her or any of the authorities. I could, at least, print in *The Florentine*, the letter that Doug wrote to the US newspapers. We found out later that this in itself instigated many calls from the readers to the various Italian agencies involved, in the hope that they might have some positive influence to bear.

What a relief when I received Mario's call the day he was released. He was completely cleared of the obstruction charges and no conditions attached to his freedom. He thanked me for my part in helping with the exposure of what had happened. Without the story getting out internationally, and particularly to the US, he doubted that he'd ever have gotten released, at least not as soon as he did.

I was shocked by what these events had taught me about Italian standards relating to both the freedom of the press and the dispensation of justice. When I later interviewed Mario for *The Florentine* I asked him why he thought the prosecutor was so intent on having him arrested and he explained that his and Doug's book had certainly cast the man in a bad light. Doug, in particular, had thought it no coincidence that the arrest had come just before its Italian publication date.

Doug's accounts of these events were printed, amongst other places, in the *Washington Post* and *The Atlantic Monthly*. A producer at *Dateline* NBC asked him and Mario to take part in a special about *The Monster of Florence,* which they did. Doug, with much trepidation, returned briefly to Italy to film the segment.

I love Florence, I love Italy, but like my feelings for my own country, I have to acknowledge, that there are parts of life there that are horrible, indefensible. The saga dragged for them both, Doug was at least safe in the US. Even after release, Mario went through depositions and trials, experiencing the drain of money and energy sucked up by a lengthy and seemingly never-ending defense. Happily, I saw Mario on a recent trip to Florence and was delighted to hear that, finally, he had been cleared of all charges.

On a more positive note, Mario continued to work for *La Nazione*, winning prizes for his writing and journalism. Mario and Doug's book spent a long time on the *New York Times* best-seller list. There's an option taken out on the movie rights too. At a personal level, Mario and Myriam are two of my closest friends in Florence; their generosity and kindness, not to mention Myriam's culinary magic, are significant reasons why I love to return to my other home.

Exchange Rates

When we started *The Florentine*, we figured that we'd need to find someone with the newspaper experience we completely lacked. We looked for a managing editor, a post for which we planned to pay a salary, no matter that we didn't know where we'd find the money to do so. When I asked a prospective candidate what would be the absolute minimum monthly amount on which she could live, I received what I thought was a very workable answer: €1500 per month. At the time this was equivalent to US$1800. Given, in my work as a consultant, my *daily* rate was higher than this, I was appreciative of the fact that the different candidates were willing to, in my opinion, work for pocket money and so practically volunteer their services. My partners had a different perspective on the salary proposed.

They hit the ceiling,

You're out of your mind! That's a fortune! She thinks you're a rich American and is taking advantage of you! There isn't even that much work to do and you're paying top dollar! We won't survive one month paying that kind of salary! And you didn't tell her it's an actual offer of employment did you?

Clearly 30 years of international management consultancy, a significant amount of it in Europe, had done little to prepare me for the *way things were done* on the employment front in Italy.

I learned a number of lessons about business and personal finance during my time in Florence. The first one was connected with my colleagues' reaction to taking on a salaried employee, basically that most businesses will not survive if they take this step. Even large corporations will do all they can to use only independent contractors so they can avoid paying out the 75% to 100% additional costs of taxes, benefits and paid vacations. Employing someone in Italy also means taking on the huge risk of never being able to fire them. Legislation is so protective of the employee that exceptionally poor performance, frequent 'sickness' and, in many instances, even theft or fraud, are no guarantee that an employer will be judged to have fairly dismissed an individual. Disputes invariably lead to settlements in favor of the employee.

When it came to *managing* finances in Florence, one of the things I was surprised to discover was how difficult it was to get money in and out of a bank! I couldn't just hand checks or cash over the counter to deposit into *The Florentine's* bank account; there had to be an invoice, a tax number, and several other documents that I still don't understand the *whys* and *wherefores* of to this day. It would make a lot more sense, if at least this cumbersome procedure only related to taking money *out,* but it was just as difficult to put money *in.* Marco held one check we received for a small advertisement for over a year, unable to pay it in, because he didn't have the *codicil fiscale* for the American woman who had sent it.

Something which affected finances at a more personal level, as well as when it came to working out what was an appropriate wage for a paid member of staff, was the lack of an obvious relationship between salaries and the cost of living. If €1500 was considered a ridiculously high salary, it would have made sense that the cost of living must have been much lower than in the US, right? But this assumption fails to take into account that Italy is the land of chaos, inconsistencies, and mysteries.

Rents, in particular are extremely high. When I had to leave my dream home on Via Ghibellina and downsize to a third floor walk-up, one bedroom apartment, a fifth of the size of where I had been, I was still faced with a rent comparable to Manhattan rates and on top of that the exorbitant cost of utilities. In Italy, you would never think of leaving a room to walk into another without turning off the light. Orientation for my visiting guests always included the instruction to take quick showers. A normal US type shower could cost me €10 each and so even a few of these would lead to a shocking utility bill at the end of the month.

There were a number of other obstacles that related to, and limited, our opportunities to make money through the paper. Presumably a very large number of creative Italians are also hindered by the same lack of incentive for entrepreneurism we experienced in Italy. Identifying, negotiating and obtaining the various licenses and permits are just the first hurdles for those wanting to run with a new business idea. Further, opportunities to secure start-up capital, through a small business loan for example, are few. And, given that the Italian market isn't known for bringing big returns on investment, it's only the bravest that would take the financial risks of giving up secure employment to develop an unproven venture.

Attempting to make *The Florentine* viable led to further frustrations when money issues combined with my partners' conservatism on the technological front. Their alleged 'mastery' in web-development did nothing to accelerate us getting *The Florentine* online - it took years, literally, and despite monthly promises that this would be achieved. I also desperately wanted us to be able to sell subscriptions and classifieds via the internet, but the guys were extremely wary of setting up online payments via credit card or *Paypal* without further investigation. It was unbelievable to me, that people had to get a money order from an Italian bank or come into the office and pay cash! I tried to explain this would not work for Americans, especially those wanting subscriptions from overseas. More incredible, however, was that while they debated and delayed, Nita, the computer illiterate, spent all of two minutes setting up *Paypal* on the blog I'd recently started! It wasn't until I'd left Italy, some four and half years after *The Florentine* started, that the guys finally took the plunge and offered online payment.

The added dimension of the way that Italy's legal history often strangles progress with the simplest of tasks, added yet more layers of complexity to attempts to be innovative. Confounding in the extreme was the cumbersome 'process' of setting up a publishing arm to *The Florentine*. From the first issue, we had featured the charming articles of Linda Falcone in which she used uniquely Italian sayings and phrases to give insights into aspects of the local culture and approach to life. I personally looked forward to each week's new piece. I met Linda for lunch to tell her of my wish to publish a compilation of her articles as a book; she was elated and agreed to the idea at once.

Again, my partners sent me bashing my head against the wall, they were totally convinced that we should not - and could not - start a publishing company. I responded that as we already published a newspaper, it would be no big deal to extend the business to include publishing books. Was I ill-informed! In Italy, for any new venture, including a flower shop owner deciding he wants to also sell greetings cards, if you haven't listed this specific item in the original paperwork, you have to either start a whole new company, or go through a mass of bureaucracy to amend your existing licenses.

In my frustration, I decided to become a publisher in the US. After five minutes and a cost of $20, I was in business, having secured 10 ISBN numbers to allocate to whatever book titles I wished. Absurdly, the same process in Italy took Marco six months, not just of waiting, but of daily form-filling and registering documents. The number of hoops through which he needed to jump, multiplied on a daily basis. It was impossible to get an upfront overview of all the requirements because, even though books have been published in Italy for centuries - we were hardly breaking new ground - there was no established protocol. One of the more bizarre steps, which we certainly never saw coming, was fulfilled when the police showed up at Marco's mother's house to get details of his family tree! In the end, before a single volume was printed, it cost us over €4000 in *commercialista* fees (for something similar to accounting/legal services) to comply with all the latest laws *and* to ensure we successfully navigated the previous 300 years of unrescinded laws that remain on the statute books.

I realised these legalities were also a source of frustration to my partners and while I got annoyed with the way they combined with the guys own cautious and conservative approach towards new endeavors, I fully acknowledge that, when it came to money-matters, it was often *me* that had *them* tearing *their* hair out. I soon found that how Italians chose to spend money - or not spend it - worked to a very different rationale than my own (or for that matter, any place else that I've ever come across in my travels). This was a real handicap for me in the business given my discovery that - whether taxes, salaries, the price of goods or utilities - nothing seemed to have equivalent values to the same things in the US. The result was, anything that I assured my partners would be a *certainty* in terms of a finance related issue such as the cost of something, an estimate of how much people would be prepared to pay for a service, or a suggestion of a *guaranteed way* to bring in income, would turn out to be a wildly inaccurate assertion. Up was down, down was up; nothing was as I thought it would be.

The question of whether or not to charge for the delivery of *The Florentine* was a typical example of me getting it wrong. In the beginning, we delivered each issue by foot and bicycle and like the newspaper itself, the delivery was *gratis*. Eventually, because we had so much demand from hotels, stores and restaurants, we needed to hire a distributor. What followed was an argument with my partners as to how to pay for this new expense. I said that we could charge the hotels a small delivery fee. Giovanni, in his predictable *è difficile* fashion, told me that the hotels would never do it and that we couldn't afford to lose the exposure their interest gave us. I countered that of course they would pay (it amounted to less than $150 a year) to ensure their guests could enjoy this service. He wouldn't budge, but after a year, when we knew that the hotels had gotten hooked on having the paper available to their guests, we finally sent out the letter announcing the minimal fee for delivery, emphasizing that there was still to be no charge for the paper itself. 90% of the hotels cancelled their order! I was shocked (though happy to report that over the next couple of years they did come back to us).

Most of all, I hated that Giovanni was right again, knowing he would add this to his growing arsenal of my *mistakes,* ever-ready to be thrown back at me on any appropriate occasion. Still, regarding money matters, there was at last a certainty on which I could come to rely: *that I would be wrong, and Giovanni would be right.*

Chic n' Cheap

Not much gives me more pleasure than shopping. My friends frequently compliment my ability to score some fabulous finds at ridiculously low prices; I've had years of practice. Florence proved a haven for honing my skills even further. I love a designer label as much as the next person, but have no qualms rejecting a famous name, even at a *you-can't-go-wrong-at-this-price* sale ticket. Similarly, if I find something bottom dollar, new or second-hand, and am impressed by the cut and material, I'm more than happy to share with incredulous friends that the latest fantastic purchase I'm showing off - whether a jacket, skirt, piece of jewelry or purse - cost me €7 from one of the markets. Putting all the pieces together for an overall look, for me or my friends, is a challenge I love. Not only do I have a good eye for what would look good on me, many of my friends will testify to the numerous times they have answered a compliment with,

Nita found this coat for me - $20 at a thrift store! It's Armani!

When it comes to productive shopping in Florence, two of my favorite places are the daily markets in Piazza Santo Spirito and Piazza Sant' Ambrogia. Both are predominantly food markets, but have tables laden with second-hand, as well as new clothes and shoes. They're open six days a week, but it can take a while to work out which stalls are there on which days, and as with all market-type goods you need patience to wade through the piles and racks. Some days you'll strike gold, others you'll leave disappointed.

One interesting feature of fashion production in Italy is that most of the clothes are made in the same factories, regardless of their price-points or designers, with some even cut from the same fabric. The Florentines are snobs about labels, and so will often pay a €1000 for an appropriately labeled pair of slacks or jacket. I have no problem buying an equally interesting piece by a no-name designer, as long as I like the style and it looks good on me. I am happy as a clam to walk away from Sant' Ambrogia with a stylish sweater or luxurious coat knowing that a factory, after fulfilling a designer's orders, has gone on to use the left-over materials to mass produce a similar style that I can pick up alongside my fresh asparagus. I have one Italian friend that practically gets mad at me,

Nita, don't tell me you bought that cashmere coat in the market! I don't believe you. It's a Prada! It has to be! I laugh,

Nope it isn't, it cost me €10, in fact I bought it in three different colors, want one?

I have scored plenty of *labels,* but usually from the second-hand tables: a vintage *Fendi* bag; an *Yves St. Laurent* sweater that my friend Natasha never takes off; several *Missoni* sweaters for Tony.

New, rather than second-hand, the San Lorenzo leather market which spans Via del Canto de'Nelli and Via dell'Ariento is one of the largest outdoor markets in Tuscany. It sells a wide variety of leather goods, coats, bags, gloves as well as scarves, stationery, clothes and shoes. Even though it's quite touristy, I still like the selection and go there to supplement my scarf collection (which I, and Italians, both men and women, wear everyday all year round). Don't forget to ask for *uno sconto.*

When it comes to proper retail stores, all the major designers can be found in the center, predominantly on Via Tornabuoni, the Rodeo Drive of Florence. But if you're looking for high fashion without the hefty price tag (think more in the €100 to €200 range), then the shops on Borgo San Jacapo are a great place to while away a few hours. Again, I wouldn't be surprised to find that many of the items are made in the same factories as their up-market cousins.

COIN, one of the two department stores in the center, at Via dei Calzauoli, is always one of my first stops upon landing in Florence; reminiscent of Bloomingdales with various, scattered departments, interesting new designers, reasonable prices. I especially like their purse department, where I purchase a wallet or bag on every trip. Not quite *Ferragamo,* but they have beautiful new styles in seasonal and unusual colors at ridiculously low prices. One of my recent purchases was a *Valentino* bag for €67. *Massimo Dutti* is another stop for me for more conservative and tailored men and women's clothing. Not really my style but it's where I get Tony's present every trip. He now has a collection of shirts and sweaters from *his* store.

A further shopping option is a day at the outlets, bus or train and taxi being the best way to get to them. Again patience is required to sift through the offerings and knowing in advance that your findings may leave you feeling anywhere from highly elated to vowing never to waste your time there again. *The Mall* and *The Space Prada* outlet are usually worth the trip, *Barabarino,* not really.

Known for my jewelry addiction, I've found a few places in Florence more in keeping with my pocket than the fabulous, though expensive, vendors on the Ponte Vecchio. A favorite discovery is *Aproiso,* in Via Santo Spirito, not least of all because of the exquisite shop, something similar to a Parisian couture house, preciously appointed. The necklaces, bracelets, brooches, earrings and bags, often featuring intricately detailed animals and flowers, are all made from crystal and glass beads. Each work of art is designed by Ornella Aprosio and makes a unique gift. Visit the website to take a look.

From my first visit to the shop, I knew I had to write an article about this treasure of a find. I tried, without success, to obtain an interview for *The Florentine* with the elusive, and I was told painfully shy, Ornella. Two weeks after being shut down again, I found myself sitting next to her at our mutual friend's country home,

You're Ornella? I've been trying to get an interview with you! I adore your jewelry, your shop, you are a maestra!

She has since become a dear friend. As well as the fortune of our friendship, I cherish the gifts she has given me, for various occasions, which adorn my wrists and ears.

L'Ocabianca at Via dei Cerchi is another good source for jewelry of contemporary design at fair prices including *Pomellato*-like pieces. *Giuseppi Calbi* at Via del Olmo, is my jewelry repairman. He also designs and fabricates his own jewelry. I can't tell you how many impulse buys I made while waiting for him to fix a clasp or replace a stone.

Gold, metaphorically and literally - is waiting to be scavenged at the various flea and antique markets where you'll find thousands of pre-loved pieces. And, not just for jewelry, Piazza dei Ciompi near Santa Croce is a great flea market held at the end of each month. In the same area there are regular stalls, open most days, selling various items from the one-time fish market. Somewhat beyond a flea market but a real must-do when in Florence, is to take the 30-minute train ride to the picturesque town of Arezzo on the first weekend of every month for the antique fair. The stalls spill through the old streets with vendors coming from all over Italy. They sell jewelry; toys; accessories; and the furniture, fixtures and fittings much sought after by interior designers looking to complete their house and business restorations and remodeling projects.

One more shopping experience I must mention, a special place for gifts, is the *Farmacia di Santa Maria Novello*. It can be found adjacent to the piazza of the same name and is one of the oldest pharmacies in the world. Officially established in 1612, its beginnings are found much earlier in the 13th century when some Dominican fathers arrived in the area and began to prepare and dispense medicine and creams from the herbs and flowers that they grew in the monastery gardens. Centuries later, in the same venue, decked out with the historic tools of the trade, Eugenio Alphandery runs the business. Many of the original formulas are used in the creation of the extensive range of homeopathic medicines, soaps, lotions and beauty products, including perfumes, all on sale today. I highly recommend a visit, if only to experience the glorious heady aromas, quite unlike those of a modern day department store perfume floor. In addition, the religious artwork and rich marbled surfaces all add to a real stepping back in time sensation.

When I return to visit Florence I hit my favorite spots with an eye to finding a treasure, or two, or three to take back to LA. There was a time, when shopping in Italy, I'd pick up unique things, leather items for example, that you wouldn't get anywhere else; this is much less the case these days with so many Italian goods being available the world over. In many ways, it's easier (and cheaper because of the great sales), to buy Italian goods in the US. The stores in Italy, due to lack of space and budget, don't usually carry as many styles and sizes as their American counterparts. Making returns is almost impossible too and if you need a different size, they wouldn't think of calling another store to obtain it for you. All that said, when it comes to shopping in Italy, I revel in the ambiance of both the stores and markets; enjoy the entertaining conversations and jokes shared with shop assistants, vendors and customers; and treasure the time and space to browse - all without which, a trip to Florence would hardly be the same.

Overflowing: The Flood Issue

When Lynn Weichmann rings the office, Giovanni always makes sure her every request is met. He either jumps into action himself or, when I am around, passes on requests to me with directions that I do whatever was required - quickly. I only wish I'd known how to cast a similar spell over Giovanni; I never seemed able to make him do anything!

I was with Giovanni when I first met Lynn and she got right to work on us,

The Florentine is amazing; this should have been done years ago; the Comune and the Region should be paying you, because you're doing their work for them, I'll talk to people and make that happen. You have to interview the sindaco (mayor) and the presidente of the Region; come to my meeting next week with the US University directors; write an article about this art exhibit; join this association; come to my house for dinner next week.

I fell in love with her energy and enthusiasm; Giovanni was merely spellbound and enslaved.

As well as becoming a wonderful advocate for *The Florentine,* Lynn, along with her husband Vieri, soon became a generous personal friend to me. I admired and respected all that she had achieved since arriving from the US for her junior year and then never leaving. She is a major force in serving the American community in Florence, all the time encouraging ex-pats and visitors to reciprocate and make a contribution to local life. Lynn was one of the founders of the International School in Florence and has held numerous civic positions in areas connected with community service. Her current incarnation is as president of the Tuscan-American Association.

Two years after our first encounter and I'm sitting with Lynn at the timelessly chic *Café Rivoire*, in Piazza Signoria overlooking the Palazzo Vecchio. She tells me about the upcoming 40th anniversary of the breaking of the banks of the Arno River and the flooding of Florence. This devastating event took place on November 4th 1966 and saw 500,000 tons of mud deposited in the city; massive landslides to the north and south; 33 deaths and the loss of thousands of homes and businesses. Countless priceless works of art were also damaged, some beyond repair.

Lynn explained that there were going to be various events to commemorate the anniversary: art exhibits; symposiums on the engineering issues (still not rectified); books published of the dramatic photographs taken at the time; and, in honor of their endeavors, the *Mud Angels* who came from all over the world to help clean up the city, were being invited to Florence. The Tuscan-American society was working on having the mayor from New Orleans (*Hurricane Katrina* had recently happened), come visit and speak.

It was then I discovered Lynn's latest mission for *The Florentine*,

Nita, I want The Florentine to put on an exhibit in the Palazzo Vecchio and you can work with the Comune and organize all the related festivities.

My first thought was relief that Giovanni had not accompanied me to this meeting; he couldn't say *no* to Lynn, but I could! Of course I listened to Lynn and thought she had some great ideas but told her that, as a newspaper, creating exhibits wasn't really *The Florentine*'s business. However, at the same time as I was resisting this request for help a light switched on in my head!

We had recently been hired to do a special edition of *The Florentine* for a commercial venture called *The Ponte Vecchio Challenge,* an event produced by various golf-related companies. Bizarre, but true, the annual event involved four professional golfers teeing off from the Ponte Vecchio, aiming to land their shots on three artificial floating islands especially created in the middle of the Arno River. Amateurs and enthusiasts are also invited to participate in the challenge and to attend the accompanying exhibits where people can find out about golf memberships, equipment, books and DVDs, tours, instruction and vacations. The hosting organization hired us to make a special edition newspaper, not part of our regular run, and more-or-less made up of advertisements. Financially, it was a great gig for us and goodness knows we needed all the help we could get on that front.

And so it had come to me that we could make a special edition of *The Florentine* to commemorate the 40th anniversary of the flood. It wouldn't be a commercial venture, but a signature way for *The Florentine* to be supportive of Lynn's efforts as well as participating in this significant event for Florence - and all in a manner that drew upon what we knew how to do. She jumped at the idea, told me she would raise the money for it (which didn't happen, but another story), and off we were.

Though a tortuous process, largely because of limited resources including finances and staff, we ended up publishing a memorable edition. The diverse and compelling content made for an issue that paid tribute to the glory of Florence and its citizens at a difficult time. The dramatic sepia photo on the front page captured the full impact of the shocking event. Inside, we included first-hand accounts of Florentines who were children at the time, one woman recalling how she climbed onto the roof with her parents; descriptions of the event from news articles of the period; original photographs and the stories of other mementos collected by the *Mud Angels* and survivors; details of the damage to paintings, statues and books and the subsequent restoration efforts; and an hour by hour account of the occurrences of that fateful day. We covered how, in addition to the brutal force of nature, human error had played a part in the escalation of the disaster. We were enormously proud of the final output and felt that it truly reflected the significance of the occasion as well as educated a new generation about the disaster.

On November 4th 2006, 40 years to the day, the special flood issue of *The Florentine* was published. Thousands of copies were distributed around the city and made available at every exhibit, lecture and event related to the anniversary. The *Comune* sent copies to Italian-American Centers and consulates all over the US. Keepsake-worthy, we soon realized we hadn't printed nearly enough. Copies are precious now and will no doubt become more so.

We were honored to be able to include a message from the now late Senator Edward Kennedy. When the disaster occurred in 1966, he was one of the first influential people to bring American money and practical aid to Florence. Along with a photo of the great man, we printed his words praising the efforts of the many *Mud Angels,* from Italy and around the world, who came together to rescue and restore many of the cultural treasures of the city. The Senator was actually going to be one of the speakers at a two-day symposium to be held at Villa La Pietra, which would cover scientific, restorative, preventive and historical issues relating to the flood.

The Saturday luncheon, when the Senator would be speaking, happened to coincide with one of my fabulous hunt weekends at Il Borro. So as not to shirk my editorial duties (or a chance to meet Ted Kennedy) I spent Friday night in the country, had breakfast with the hunters, and then drove back into town. Once again, I pinched myself to remember that this was actually *my* life I was living.

The Senator started his talk by saying that on the day of the flood, he got a call from *Jackie, my sister-in-law*, who had implored,

Teddy, I'm worried about my Florence, you have to go there!

He arrived in Florence the next day, and described to us what it looked like to see such a magnificent jewel drowning under water. Senator Kennedy returned to the US to rally for help. He said he'd known that young Americans responded with vigor to situations that immediately affected their own country such as civil rights and involvement in war, but that he'd had no idea what their reaction to a plea to help in far away Florence would be; especially when it was works of art rather than lives that were in need of rescue. He confirmed what we now knew, that the response had been tremendous. Along with Italians and many other nationalities, American students, professors, art experts and restorers arrived in Florence in droves, wading through the mud, working in the mud, sleeping in the mud and truly earning their moniker, the *Mud Angels*. These cleaning and restoration efforts were funded by US banks giving no-interest loans. The Senator said he was happy to acknowledge that once again Americans had shown up where they were needed.

Ellyn Toscano, director of Villa La Pietra and host of the event, came and got me from my table,

Nita, you *have to talk to Ted, go!*

She moved over one of the other guests who had been seated next to him and introduced me. I took out the special edition of *The Florentine* which he had yet to see, showed him the issue, and thanked him for his message, his enormous contribution to Florence, and his unrelenting work in the US Senate. He had just won the election which had also brought the Democrats into majority in Congress. He was very impressed with the paper, exclaiming at the photos and complimenting me on the issue. I was well aware I shouldn't linger too long at my privileged audience and I was about to take leave, when my arm was grabbed by a woman who turned out to be a close friend of the Kennedy's and part of the Senator's accompanying group. She said she had seen me speaking with La Signora Wanda Ferragamo, who was seated at the Senator's table and asked me if she spoke English as she wanted to tell her something. I explained that Wanda spoke beautiful English, but she still insisted I introduce her.

My role of interpreter (not that I was really needed in this capacity) allowed me access to a precious story. The American woman told Wanda that her son was born with one leg shorter than the other. She explained that many years earlier, on reading that Salvatore Ferragamo had designed himself a special pair of shoes, to accommodate an injury following a car accident, she had written to tell him about her son. The founder of the *Ferragamo* business had written her back, requesting the various measurements of her son's feet and legs. After a short while, he sent her son a pair of shoes, customized to his exact needs, along with instructions to re-send the measurements every year so that he could make new ones as her son's feet grew. Wanda grabbed the woman's hand, she was in tears. She confided that apparently her husband had done many things like this, but she probably hadn't heard the half of them.

Wanda thanked me profusely for bringing the woman to her; the American woman hugged me for giving her the opportunity to thank La Signora Ferragamo; Senator Kennedy had thanked me for my part in making such an incredible tribute to what Florence had experienced 40 years ago. I was humbled. How could these extraordinary people be thanking me? It was me who was overflowing with gratitude as I drove back to re-join the other Ferragamos at the hunt party.

When I heard the news that Ted Kennedy had died, I brought out the photos taken at the luncheon. There we are, Ted and I. I am showing him the copy of *The Florentine*.

May he rest in peace.

Lessons in Perspective

In the fall of 2007, I received two pieces of news that rocked my universe: Montana, my 18 year old daughter had gotten married (we were talking a lot during this time but she'd planned the wedding without Tony or me and nor were we invited); and that the girlfriend of my 23 year old son, Jordan, was pregnant. In a completely different context - if they'd been much older - I'd have been delighted by such news! I have to say that neither event gave me the slightest joy. I was actually devastated by both.

My feelings were intense: shame, embarrassment, fear and despair. Despite others assuring me that this was not my fault, I felt defeated and a failure as a mother. I immediately set about making these things all about me, and the realization I was doing this further fueled my self-condemnation. I went first to this negative place. However, prolonged self-pity is not my style. I knew I had to do something to put things into perspective.

I got myself clear on a few facts. *My children are alive, healthy and still as wonderful as ever; I talk to them both almost every day, despite our distance, and our relationships are strong and loving. They haven't destroyed their lives with their choices, they've changed their lives.* I also recognized that in a very profound way, these choices would, in fact, bring them insight. OK, I can't brag that my son is in medical school or that my daughter goes to Julliard. So what? It isn't about me. I'll get over it.

Some few weeks following both pieces of news, I was busy on *The Florentine* but accepted two invitations from US friends to visit them while they were in Europe. One friend, Ronni Chasen, was in Paris and had the use of a luxurious apartment. I put myself in her hands, and spent three days going out to lunch and dinner with her Parisian friends, mostly ex-pats. My friend is a big Hollywood publicist and her Paris crowd consisted of mostly wealthy people in the design industry. All of them were lovely, generous and included me in their invites to chic events and trendy restaurants.

Usually, I can hold my own in any group of people. My experience with *The Florentine* had given me numerous opportunities to socialize with diplomats, politicians, teachers, Italian nobility and major designers. But I realized after a couple of days in Paris, that no one amongst this group of people was even vaguely interested in me. And probably, for the first time in my life, I felt that the reason for this was that I wasn't rich or famous enough to be *one of them*. My reaction was more a feeling of surprise rather than rejection. I certainly didn't feel like I was less than them in any way. I still enjoyed myself that weekend, but it was a baffling experience for me.

The following weekend couldn't have been more different than my time in Paris. My dear friend, Debra McGuire, who I've known for more than 40 years, had some work in Munich and suggested I meet her there for the weekend. Debra is a costume designer, her credits include many ground-breaking TV shows such as *Friends* and *Heroes* and movies including *Anchorman*, *40 Year Old Virgin* and

Knocked Up. At the time she was working on a film with Robert DiNiro and Al Pacino. In between TV and film work she went to Munich to sell a line of her clothing designs on *Home Shopping Europa*, the German version of *Home Shopping Network.*

That Friday, I went directly from the airport in Munich to meet her at the TV studio and watch her shoot two shows. It was a kick! Debra spoke in English, her host in German. Clothes, fashion, models and TV cameras, I loved being a backstage witness to it all.

Back at the hotel, we talked until the early hours, two girls having a sleepover. I spent a lot of time crying about my children - the wedding, the pregnancy. With children of her own, she commiserated with the aches and pains as well as sharing in the joys of motherhood. Crying and laughing about our children, comparing their escapades to those of our own in our more youthful years, we also swapped stories about the other stages of our lives that had led to this moment, two friends in a Munich hotel bedroom.

When she knew I was coming to visit her in Germany, Debra told me that for some time she'd wanted to visit the concentration camp at Dachau, but just didn't feel she had the strength to go alone. I agreed to accompany her, and on Saturday morning we made our way there. The contrast between the superficiality of our frivolous but fun Friday at the TV studios, and the dark and incomprehensible experience of a visit to Dachau, was striking.

Debra and I are Jewish. We are both known to cry very easily. Our sons, when they heard where we were going, warned us to take plenty of Kleenex, but neither of us shed a tear that day. Later, we searched for words to describe how we'd felt: *numb, stunned* and *cold.* The most difficult part for me was not, as I expected, the knowledge that such atrocities were done to people *just like us*, as in *Jewish people,* but that the atrocities were *committed by people… human beings, just like us.*

Before this visit I, like many others, thought that the German guards and soldiers used the justification of having to follow orders as an explanation of the atrocities they committed. The thought-provoking insights of the gifted guide who led us, challenged me to look deeper into this rationale and into myself. Certainly, some of the people responsible for the mass torture and systemized cleansing were out-and-out evil, but I believe the majority were not. But was this majority really just carrying out these monstrosities because they were given orders to follow? Most of these people, I reflected, were human beings with intelligence, people who had been living *normal* lives before the war started; people probably trying to do right by their kids and loved ones. As I read the letters on display, I began to see that these people really thought, by eliminating the Jews and others, they were making Germany a better place for their children. They saw the Jews as having too much control, too much money, too much education and dominating the banking, medical and legal professions. They blamed the Jews for their own lack of money and opportunity, and the less than bright future their children faced. As a mother, I know I would do anything for my children. If I thought it would benefit my children, would I do *this?*

Whatever the reasons people acted, and however misguided they were in their rationale, the realization that people can lose their humanity to such an extent that they can go through the mechanics of keeping charts to record the efficiency with which they kill people, or to calculate the cost/benefit ratio of feeding a worker versus killing him was deeply, deeply shocking. What was even more shocking was to realize, this wasn't just history - that there are similar *justifications* and *rationalizations* that argue for, and allow, torture and brutality across the world *today* even within societies with governments deemed as 'civilized' - including the US.

The mixed experiences of these two weekends with my friends in Europe fed into the personal drama of, and self-reflection on, my role as a mother. They actually created a new context for looking at the recent passages in the lives of my son and daughter. My focus shifted away from me and outwards to the feelings of love, appreciation and gratefulness that I have for my life and those within it. My children are alive; they love and are loved; they are both able to look forward to the next day with hope and they have the luxury of being free to make choices. The prisoners in the camps, as well as in many places in the world today, do not have this freedom to choose. Whatever the outcomes of my children's choices prove to be, the fact that they are free to make them is something to be celebrated.

Shame on me that I would look at their lives and feel sorry for myself...

Never in My Wildest Dreams

On September 27th 2007, I was in the office when some-one handed me an envelope. It looked like an invitation. It was a daily occurrence for me to receive invites at *The Florentine:* for openings, symposiums, press conferences and so I was expecting something along those lines. Imagine my surprise at reading the first line of the elegantly printed card: *HRH Prince of Wales invites you to Buckingham Palace.*

We'd been working on a special edition of *The Florentine* commemorating the 90th anniversary of the British Institute in Florence. I'd been told that there would be a celebratory reception in London but had no idea that it would be held in the Queen's Gallery of Buckingham Palace, or that Prince Charles would be the host.

My first thought was, *I wish my mother was alive. Who would get more out of this honor than even me, but my mother?*

The next thought, of course, was: *what am I going to wear?*

Fortunately I had a few contacts to ask for advice. My girlfriend Patty Detroit had worked with Oscar winning writer Sir Julian Fellowes. He is married to Lady Emma Fellowes, lady in waiting to Princess Michael of Kent. Via Patty, I received the following e-mail from Sir Julian:

Emma is in Bruges, but I have been to these things, and I know that she (Nita) has to wear what used to be called a 'smart cocktail' dress. Not long, but not informal. The gallery (where the event was being held) *is very beautiful and was rebuilt not all that long ago. It is part of the Palace, and, in fact, is on the site of the chapel that was bombed in the Blitz ("Now we can look the East End in the face."). She will enjoy herself. If she does get presented to the Prince, she should remember that the grander the lady the lower the curtsey. Servants bob. Ladies curtsey.*

Love, Julian

And in response to a similar request for information on dress etiquette for the occasion my friend William sent this:

I would guess that it would be cocktail dress, or some would be coming from work so would be wearing something slightly more business. The men would be in lounge suits i.e. smart informal, not black tie or anything like that (unless of course one is going on to such an event afterwards). You can practice your curtsey next time you see me!

William, aka Lorde of Seaforde in the County of Down, Ulster (but also peasant from Ennis, County Clare, Munster), all in ye islande of Irelande.

I started the search in my closet, where I rediscovered a stunning *Armani* evening suit (I know not a dress, but I was sure it would fit the bill) that I purchased on a trip to Florence 20 years ago. It fit, and was beautiful, and I realized that if I were to go shopping that very day, I would choose the same thing. I also had the perfect pair of *Prada* heels, bought five years ago, and never worn, and a vintage *Balenciaga* purse. *Fortunately,* I didn't have to buy a thing. *Unfortunately,* I didn't get to buy a thing!

My friend, Ellyn Toscano, was also invited, so we planned a three-day trip to London together. We arrived the Monday and started things off with a visit to the theatre. A few months before, Ellyn had hosted some English actors at the Villa La Pietra and they'd read through *The Giant*, Anthony Sher's play about the sculpting of *David*. Despite the play's less than great reviews and much needed edit, I thoroughly enjoyed the performance, not only because the acting was superb, but because I knew all the actors. After the performance, the man himself, Leonardo *aka* Roger Allam, and his friend, took Ellyn and me out to dinner at a very *in* place, *The Woolsey*. I was, of course, in heaven: a hip venue; dining with well-known actors and on top of all that, enjoying intelligent, stimulating and witty conversation.

Next morning, we passed the day looking for an evening bag for Ellyn, running around London only to find cheap *shlock* or frighteningly expensive beauties. Finally at 4.00pm, we gave up, and went to get our nails and hair handled for the evening. We parted with small fortunes for a wash, blow dry and manicure, but how many times do you get the chance to posh-up for a *do* at Buckingham Palace?

We arrived on time for the two-hour reception at 6.00pm. Once inside I asked one of the governors of the British Institute if I would be allowed to get a photo with *The Prince*. He told me that, as it was considered a private engagement, no press or photos were allowed. In fact, he noted that I was the only journalist there. What a rare privilege!

Prince Charles is one of the patrons of the British Institute in Florence as is Wanda Ferragamo. To mark the occasion of its 90th anniversary, the Italian component of the British monarchy's considerable private art collection was on display in the Queen's Gallery; getting to view this was worth the trip alone. Not only were the works individual masterpieces but every single painting had been impeccably restored to an exquisite condition. There were paintings by Titian, Artemisia, Canaletto and two extraordinary canvases by Caravaggio.

I was surprised at how many people I knew at the event; people I'd interviewed during my time at *The Florentine* including several members of Florence's noble families such as the Corsini, Frescobaldi, della Gheradesca, and also, the president of the *Region* and assistant mayor. I was eager to greet all of these friends but also enjoyed working the room to meet as many new people as I could.

Without any pomp or circumstance, Prince Charles appeared in the middle of the gallery. I waited my turn to meet him. Our conversation went something like this:

Nita: *I'm the editor-in-chief of The Florentine, the newspaper in Florence. We are the ones who produced the special issue for this 90th anniversary (a copy was included in the gift bags given to each guest).*

HRH: *Thank you so much for doing that, I perused the issue earlier, it's beautifully done.*

Nita: *Thank you for the great honor of your invitation. This exhibit is amazing. The paintings are in such beautiful condition, impeccably restored.*

HRH: *I know, and did you see the Caravaggio over there? It was in such awful shape, and so dark that we didn't even know it was a Caravaggio until a few years ago.*

Nita: *And how did you discover that it was authentic?*

HRH: *It was a man named Maurizio…?* (He turned to his assistant*)*

Nita: *Oh, Maurizio Seracini. Yes, I know him well, in fact we are about to publish a book about the search for the 'Lost Leonardo' in the Palazzo Vecchio; Maurizio is a key player in developing the technology involved in attempting to uncover it.*

HRH: *That's such a fascinating project.*

Well, I was a bit blown away that I'd found myself quite at ease talking art authentication with HRH Prince Charles! Charming isn't the right word to describe him, more like gracious in a very effortless and engaging way. When I later shared with Montana how easy it was to have a conversation with him, she said,

Mom, he's been trained to be that way his whole life.

Well, she may be right, but credit given where credit's due; he still does it well.

The event over, I went to retrieve my coat from the coat check. I noticed in front of me, a very attractive blond woman in a particularly stunning dress. I looked at her face, and asked,

Are you Trudie?

And yes, it was Trudie Styler, Sting's wife! I thought it best not to begin the conversation with *I'm totally in love with your husband* and, instead, mentioned *The Florentine* as well as showing her his picture in that very issue (an article about Brits throughout history finding a home in Italy, titled *From Shelley to Sting)*. I told her that Sting was actually our first subscriber and I was dying to get an interview with him. She said that maybe it would be possible when he returned from his tour with *The Police*.

The glamour and glitz didn't end at the gates of *The Palace*. As we were leaving we bumped into Princess Giorgina Corsina. I knew her from various events in Florence as well as having interviewed her. She invited Ellyn and me to dinner at her friend's house in Belgravia. And there we were: one Princess; two Marchesas; a Countess; the wonderful Ellyn from Brooklyn; and Nita living-a-fairytale from Detroit.

The fun continued the next day when we enjoyed the delightful company of Sir Julian Fellowes and his wife, Lady Emma to whom Patty had kindly introduced us via e-mail.

What a couple; Julian, dapper and dignified and Emma, a six-foot beauty, statuesque, gorgeous, dramatic and clearly moving in the most refined circles and enjoying the privileges of her role. They were both charming hosts and as we, and they, had planned to head to see a fashion exhibit at The Victoria and Albert Museum after breakfast, we all went together. Julian, enjoying huge success from his theatrical adaptation of Mary Poppins, was currently writing a musical play about Christian Dior and he was going back to see the exhibit for the third time for his research. Our trip through the museum was greatly enhanced by their historical snippets and fashion anecdotes. Emma pointed out on which dress she modeled her Oscar gown and the style of hats she had to have,

They must be simply huge…because I am so tall.

And then I was back in the hotel to retrieve my luggage. I walked to the tube, dragging my suitcase behind me; it was the cheapest way to get my bargain flight back to Florence. Once again I found myself laughing at the contrast of it all and filled with warmth and gratitude for the wonderful and generous friends I had, and all the connections that Florence and *The Florentine* had brought me. I came from a very comfortable upper middle-class family and thankfully my parents helped me develop the confidence to believe that I could do anything, or be whatever I wanted…but somehow, I still never, ever, imagined that one day I would be chatting with Prince Charles about a Caravaggio.

Return on Investment

How did you support yourself while you were in Florence? How did you pay for it? Everyone wants to know the answers. Money, or rather lack of it, is often what people *say* gets in the way of them pursuing their dreams. I'm not sure it always *is* the real issue. Anyway, lack of money didn't get in the way for me in Florence; though lack it I certainly did! This is not a *how-to* story. My general modus operandi is always *just do it* but I don't advise everyone to follow my path; my adventure was done without a safety net and not for the faint-hearted. I repeat - *do not try this at home!*

We came to Italy with enough money to last for, we estimated, anywhere between two and four years; it lasted ten months. *The Florentine* never generated money to pay us, as the owners, salaries or profits; the cash-flow always going in the other direction with *us* regularly 'feeding' the paper.

As far as seeking to earn money in Florence by means other than through the newspaper, my experienced ex-pat friends shared the following, what I was to learn to be truths:
1) How do you leave Florence with two million dollars? Come with five million!
2) If you want to make money while you live in Florence, then have a business or investments in the US and go back and forth, much easier than investing in a business and trying to make it work in Italy.

3) If you want to work for someone else in Italy, this requires overcoming many and massive hurdles, even to be a waitress or work in a clothing store, you need a *partita iva,* working visas and other documents - and the process of obtaining them is mysterious, difficult and expensive.

4) While you could consider the possibility of working *nero,* black, the Italian expression for *under the table,* you certainly won't earn much this way and there'll be legal risks attached for you and your employer.

5) One of the few legitimate ways to make enough money to survive in Florence is to find employment with a US or global company, or a university.

Yet, none of these significant things were my own hurdles to finding paid employment; I simply had no interest in looking outside of what I considered my real job. I'd stayed in Florence because of *The Florentine.* My work on the paper consumed my time and energy and I was passionate about the difference I was making through my efforts. Most significantly, I loved every minute of what my work entailed.

When Tony returned to the US, he bought into a business in LA (a city where neither of us had ever lived) that did marble and masonry restoration. He began to make an income. The plain facts of the matter were that Tony felt he needed to live in the smallest, cheapest place he could find and take a monk's vow of poverty so that Montana and I could continue to live like princesses in our *Palazzo Ferragamo* (I did, later, when Montana left, downsize). Still, even if he could have found somewhere better to live than his one room tear-down, it's true he wasn't earning enough to support two rents, car payments in two continents, a private school for Montana and the money required to pay the salaries, meager though they were, for those few paid jobs on *The Florentine.*

Now that I'm earning a good living myself working as a consultant back in LA, people ask me why we can't afford to buy our own home, or how I always seem to be broke. The answer is simple: I'm paying off the credit cards that I lived off of for three years in Florence. Was it responsible? Was it a smart way to live? Not by many people's standards, but it would be a complete lie if I said I had a single regret about it, or that I wouldn't do it all over again in a New York minute. Would I recommend anyone else to fund their dream this way? Well, all I can say is it's a very personal decision and clearly not a strategy for everyone. You'd need to weigh how comfortable you'd be living with the debt as it built up, as well as with the consequences that resulted from having to pay it back. If I had waited until I had saved the money or secured a job before I moved to Italy, it wouldn't have happened - and if my 50th birthday was bad, my 60th would have felt like a death-march! For me, it was a risk I *had* to take.

You may have concluded that Tony had a somewhat different view of the situation than me and yes *stupid* and *irresponsible* were words he applied to the way money poured out of our bank account with *nothing to show for it*. But, life is strange. In 2009, the financial collapse in the US led to the plummeting values of people's homes and stock investments. In LA, the home foreclosure rates were the highest in the country. Everyone we knew had lost most, or at least a huge amount, of their financial net worth.

We were having several people at our home for a Shabbat dinner. One of our traditions is to ask each person at the table to say three things about the preceding week for which they were grateful. Tony shocked me by saying,

If we had done with our money what I thought we should have done, owned a home and other investments, we would have lost it all, and been pretty broke right now. We didn't lose a penny in this crash, although we are still pretty broke. However, we have no money because we spent it all on trips all over the world with the family and living in Italy. At least we had a ball losing our fortune! I'm grateful that maybe Nita had the right idea after all...

After 28 years of marriage, the man can still blow me away!

Across the Universe

When I was fortunate to meet the much lauded writer and musician Leonard Cohen, on a trip back to the US, I told him that for me, his lyrics, poetry and music were like a bridge that crossed a gap somewhere between words and the divine. He laughed,

Yes, every once in a while, you just stumble upon it.

In Florence, *stumbling upon* art that emotionally moved me, or challenged my thinking, was a regular occurrence: paintings, sculpture, theatre, music, film or some other surprising medium. And yet, even amongst such a wealth of historic awe inspiring creativity, now and again, something new would stand out and I could see from my own reaction and that of those around me, that a piece of art or an artistic event, had truly tapped into some universal aspect of what it is to be human.

Every year Italy observes a day of memoriam for the victims of the holocaust. During my tenure at *The Florentine* I attended numerous events attached to this day of remembrance. The most memorable of these, not least of all because I was a participant rather than solely a spectator, was a staged play reading by the Florence International Theatre Company. The drama told of a small town in Poland in the 1940s where the Jewish people knew that the time would soon come, when they would be taken from their homes and into the ghetto to suffer the same fate as so many of their faith and kin. To escape capture they headed for the sewers, creating a life for themselves in an underground world.

The compelling story, *Sewers of L'vov*, based on true events, was the work of a class of 13 year-olds from New Jersey and was directed by a friend, and the founder of FITC, Bari Hochwald. It was performed at the Florence Synagogue. The diverse cast included young Italian kids; American college students; some of my Italian friends; amateur actors from Italy, India, the UK and US; elders of the synagogue; and others, like me, from a small contingent of *anyone else off the street*.

We read from the scripts held in our hands, and acted out basic stage directions; the lack of backdrops and props added a fitting starkness to the story, intensifying the focus on the lives and emotions of those whose experience was being shared and explored. It wouldn't do the play and the performance justice to describe it as something *cross-cultural* or *ecumenical* or *inter-faith*. Such terms draw upon *differences*, albeit the coming together of those that are, indeed, different. For me, the power of the event came from the *universal* elements of being human into which it tapped, and the way it allowed us to experience and confront them together: fear, love, the will to survive, the need to hope. The atmosphere was charged; the participants and audience touched by feelings that lay at the very core of humanity, the place where we are all alike.

I was still reeling from the impact of that special evening, when I attended a concert hosted by the US Consul General, Nora Dempsey. A beautiful and talented singer herself, she has used music as a way of promoting cultural understanding and collaboration throughout the world. She describes music as a language of diplomacy, a method of communication that *inspires*, rather than *demands*, respect, admiration, and appreciation between those of different cultures and backgrounds. While on a previous diplomatic assignment in Tunisia, Nora befriended a local musician, Riadh Fehri, whom she then introduced to her US colleague Brennan Gilmore, a maestro of the American bluegrass tradition. Their union created a joyous and energizing *mishmash* of style and talent.

The concert I attended in Florence was part of the duo's European and African tour. The audience included the President of the Province; the Mayor of Pontassieve; the Iman of Florence; a world-study group from General Electric and; several international journalists. It was impossible not to get caught up in the music, everyone clapping, dancing and laughing to the infectious rhythm. Riadh ran us through the members of the band and, clearly moved by the mood of the audience, in tears he introduced,

My brother, Brennan Gilmore!

Once again it wasn't the *multicultural* or *interfaith* dimensions of this evening that stood out; this was no African-American, or Muslim-Christian event. Art, this time in the shape of incredible, uplifting and inspiring music, had successfully conjured up a peek into a possible future. The buzz of energy, creativity and joy had connected us to a universal and deeply human hope: to live in peace and understanding.

How Not to Screw It Up

If it wasn't how I managed financially in Florence that's most on people's minds when they hear my tale, it's how did my marriage survive after Tony left and went back to the US while I stayed in Florence another three years? Well, clearly Tony is no ordinary husband, but there's no doubt that the situation put an incredible strain on our relationship. It was the only time we've ever come close to splitting up. The stress came not just from having long periods apart, but having to re-identify and discover ourselves as individuals after 25 years as a couple. What began to reveal itself at this time was an unhealthy aspect of our relationship, of which we hadn't been consciously aware as things were so good between us. If this hadn't uncovered itself at this time, maybe, like an untreated low-grade infection, it might have eventually erupted in a more virulent and possibly incurable form.

Not only have Tony and I always been committed to each other, one of the magical ingredients to our relationship has been that we are committed to each other's sense of fulfillment, satisfaction, passion and excitement. This has never involved compromise and trade-offs such as one of us only getting to do, or have something, if another gets the equivalent. So, when Tony brought up going back to the US, I knew it was something he felt *he* had to do. I didn't take it personally. I also knew it wasn't something that I felt

I needed to do. Even though the paper wasn't financially viable, I felt a responsibility for it; I was needed in Florence and it was where I wanted to be. I think he wanted me to feel the same financial obligation or imperative to return to the US with him, or to beg him to stay with me in Florence. I did neither, but I did support his decision to go back. That didn't mean the day he left Florence wasn't devastating for me... and for him.

Tony returned to the US. He went to Seattle and then Santa Fe and after receiving job offers in both places, ended up buying into the perfect business for him in LA. He loved his work, but I still don't think I can imagine the depth and pain of his loneliness, being without me and his daughter. Although we have many friends in LA, he didn't connect with them. He was lonely, miserable, ashamed and embarrassed that his wife was not with him. He didn't want to be a *third wheel* having dinner with other couples. Friends called to play golf or have dinner, but he found it very difficult to get out of his slump. And his gloom was exacerbated by his attitude, that because I was spending money in Italy, he felt he had to get the cheapest, tiniest place to live, drive an old car and live on pizza and other fast food.

Meanwhile I was living *la dolce vita*. Though I missed Tony terribly, being without him in Florence was, in many ways, much easier for me without him there. My Italian was considerably better than Tony's and, much more out-going by nature, the whole meeting and getting to know people was a comfortable activity for me. Tony liked quiet time and at least some nights in; when out, he struggled to catch the drift of conversations and make as many connections. With Tony back in the US, I took advantage of the opportunity to go out every night. Since Montana was fiercely independent and only wanted to hang with her own friends, I could easily respond to spur of the moment invitations and not feel that I was neglecting her, or indeed Tony. I felt like I had the best of both worlds. I relished in the security of having a loving, stable relationship, I talked to Tony every night and we saw each other every six to eight weeks and, at the same time, I could be a free spirit. Though, to be explicit, the latter did not include enjoying, or seeking, any romantic connections! Many have wondered, about my being alone amongst these infamous Casanova's,

You must have gotten numerous offers of 'amore' from these gorgeous Florentine men?

The *honest* truth is in four years, I never said *yes* to any advances; the *sad* truth is I never got an opportunity to say *no!* Basically, I was quite content with the bi-continental arrangement. Tony was miserable.

Conventional wisdom, would of course dictate that, given that I loved and was committed to this man, I should have gone back to LA. I certainly knew what others thought, the judgments they were making, and probably even what people may think when they read this. But something in me listened for a deeper truth.

Our relationship began to unravel when Tony started holding me responsible for his misery. Our phone calls were often difficult. I would look forward to sharing my day with him, the excitement, coincidences, things that had happened to me, but he would go silent and grumpy. I eventually stopped wanting to share the wonders of my life with him, because it would evolve into an argument or at least a dampening of my experience. Still, there were occasional glimpses of the humor for which I loved him, even if wrapped in unhappiness,

Nita, I just want to know if you are planning on coming back here on a permanent basis. Because if you're not, then it's really not the kind of marriage I want to have. And if I'm going to have to find a new relationship, I need to know quickly. I'm

not rich and powerful enough to find a woman when I'm an old fart, I need to find one now before I start drooling!

I started down-playing any good news when I called Tony. It felt like he was jealous of the newspaper as well as my life in Florence and for the first time ever in our relationship, he resented my happiness. Who wanted to be with someone who doesn't want you to be happy? *This is not Tony, this is not our marriage!* There were some awful trips when I came back to the US when he'd be mad from the moment I arrived. Why would I give up my life in Florence to be with this angry, and therefore not particularly attractive, person? In my book: *How Not To Screw It Up: 10 Steps to an Extraordinary Relationship*, I advise how critical it is to bring your happiness *to* a relationship and not to make that relationship responsible *for* your happiness; I was getting a powerful reminder about why that was so important.

Not many people understood me then, or probably now, I realize that. Without a shadow of a doubt, I know that if my husband had *needed* me to go back to LA, a serious health issue or an accident for example, then I would have headed back in a second. But this wasn't a real need, it was a co-dependency. My returning to Tony at that time would have made this worse and that wouldn't have worked for anyone.

During one of my trips to LA, on my birthday actually, Tony said he wanted a divorce. It was the lowest point of our marriage. A true friend, who didn't have her own agenda on how marriages *should be*, challenged me,

Is your marriage worth fighting for? I knew the answer and in response to his request for a divorce told Tony that we had something incredible, something extraordinary and I wasn't willing to give up on it. I think this was what he needed to hear from me, and I certainly hadn't been saying it enough.

I loved being in LA for the several months a year I was there, and I also loved being in Florence. I would have been happy living this way indefinitely, but Tony couldn't. Then we had a turning point in our relationship. Tony came to Europe to take a vacation with me. We went for a week in Croatia, just the two of us. From our first trip together trekking for three weeks in Nepal, after only knowing each other for a few months, we've traveled well together; we're *us* at our best. We love adventures, surprises, and have always had a ball together and Croatia was no exception. Then Tony came back to Florence with me for a few days before returning to LA. He was there to celebrate the three year birthday of *The Florentine* and able to receive the acknowledgment and appreciation for what, after all, was his idea.

Later, I heard that at the party, he'd told my friend Jody it was really fun for him having me in Italy and being able to come visit me and for us to travel together and how much he loved *The Florentine*. Our relationship transformed; this was followed by an incredible summer with Tony in LA.

When I was waiting the arrival of my new grandson, I realized that I just couldn't imagine myself living that far away from this new addition to our family. My grandchild would be living in Florida, Tony in LA. How could I be in LA on one of my visits back to the US and then get on an airplane to anywhere other than Florida to see my grandson? This pull was already over-powering and Luca hadn't even been born yet!

I decided to move back.

In terms of what this meant for my relationship with Tony, the stars had aligned. I don't think it was a coincidence that once it had become alright with Tony that I was there in Florence and he supported my accomplishments, my work and my happiness, that suddenly I was making plans to return home and live with him again.

That summer Tony told me that going to LA and starting over by himself was the hardest thing he had ever done in his life, and that it was also the best thing he had ever done. Before he met me, Tony was very independent and able to take care of himself in all ways, not just financially. He had a great network of friends, arranged social activities, took trips, found jobs and took classes on his own. When we got together, I took over more and more of the organization of these things, especially socially, and it's as if he forgot he was still capable of doing this for himself. When he got to LA, Tony had no life, and started blaming me. Finally, he got it together, joined a tennis group, starting having dinner with friends, went to movies by himself, did things with the kids, began taking care of himself, and, once again, remembered who he was.

An even more serendipitous and, I would venture to say, *transformational*, result of our separation was connected to Tony's tendency to worry, or get down about situations, financial as well as personal and family things. My job, or what I had taken on as my job, was to talk him out of this worry by convincing him that we could handle it, work through a plan, and build his confidence that things would be ok. Since I had so much going on myself in Florence, as well as being somewhat resentful and sick of *his problems* (which were seemingly all my fault), I just stopped being there for him in this way. Just like in his social life, Tony began to handle this stuff himself. When he goes through similar moods now, where before I used to feel like I had to take care of it for him, now I'll just say I'm sorry he's feeling upset, and within minutes, he snaps out of it.

And so, back living together again, with both our kids out on their own we're empty-nesters a bit earlier than we planned. Like many couples who had spent the years together with kids in the house, we didn't know what it would be like to be just the two of us. It's a blast! I feel loved, and secure, and we have lots of fun doing stuff together. There are also many things we do on our own and we do these comfortably without either of us feeling rejected in any way. I continue being very social, going to plays, parties, belonging to a book club; I don't mind going out on *school nights*. Tony isn't a hermit, but happy not to go out every night, he'll often ask:

Do I have to go?

Usually, the answer is *no*. I don't get embarrassed it being just me with other couples, nor do I feel like I have to make excuses for Tony.

How did our relationship not merely survive but ultimately thrive through these trials and tribulations, challenges and growth? I used to think it was because I followed all the insightful and wise advice I gave others in my relationship books. Now, I think the real answer is that I just lucked out and married the greatest man around.

Feeding the Inner Tuscan

Italy, as my friends often reminded me, was relatively wasted on me from a *foodie* perspective. I love food and have a healthy appetite; it's just that I don't seem to be as discriminating or appreciative of flavors, cooking techniques and presentation as many of my friends. I'm more or less famous for not spending time in the kitchen. I do, however, love the social activity surrounding the consumption of food and wine. And of course, in Florence, there's the fact that the experience of wining and dining will mean that, more often than not, you'll find yourself in incomparably picturesque surroundings, frequently enjoying a romantic vista.

I am delighted when good food just appears in front of me and, happily, during my time at *The Florentine* it often did. Invitations to fashion shows, book signings, art exhibits and store openings gave me the opportunity to indulge in the delicious spreads of cheese, meat, bread and olives offered alongside the wine and cocktails. There were also the more formal events to attend such as a masquerade ball at the US Consulate or the hunt ball with the Ferragamos at Il Borro; these always involved sumptuous offerings of Italian, and regional food.

Olive oil and bread are staples of a Tuscan diet, the local versions of the former being spectacular and, for my taste, the latter less so; Tuscan bread is notoriously dry. The salt that once entered the region through the port at Pisa was, long ago, subject to a hefty tax that saw its removal from the bakers' list of essential ingredients. The tax is no longer an issue but the tradition lives on and the result is bread with a short shelf-life and a challenging texture (though favored by the Tuscans). Fortunately, alternatives were available for me to dip into the luscious, local olive oil.

A food story that also involved adapting to straightened circumstances, though with a much happier ending for me, is that of the invention of Pietro Ferrero. During WWII, this patisserie maker got around the rationing of cocoa beans by supplementing his limited supply with toasted hazelnuts, resulting in what was to become a big favorite of mine - *Nutella*! Who says I'm not a foodie?

One thing I love about food in Italy, is the fact that, much more so than in the US, it's very clearly the time of year that determines what people eat at home and what is on the menu at a restaurant. In-season, and therefore fresh, good quality (and mainly local) fruits and vegetables dictate the dishes available. I interviewed several chefs while working on *The Florentine* and soon got to understand their look of confusion when I asked their favorite dishes to cook; there was no one simple answer to the question, as the response, of course, would depend on the month you were asking them.

At lunchtime, even on a working day, for Italians, *Il Pranzo* means sitting down at a table, whether at home or at a restaurant. Traditionally, and still in the countryside and smaller towns, everyone goes home part way through the day to eat and rest. Even in Florence, other than in the tourist center, most stores and businesses close for lunch from somewhere between 1:30pm and 5.00pm. However, given that many people now work too far away from home to make a midday return visit convenient, the *popolo*, or working class people, head to a *trattoria* for lunch. A special, or *tavola calda,* is available each day at an economical price with maybe pasta, risotto or gnocchi followed by a stew or grilled meat with vegetables.

People head to the same *trattoria* every day, recreating the sense of belonging that the family table brings, getting to know those who serve and cook for them. Staff and customers alike pass jokes, share gossip and update each other on family life, also discussing the menu and their likes and dislikes about the dishes and the way they are cooked.

The guys from *The Florentine* had *their place* for lunch, one block away from work. If I came to the office and found out they were at lunch, I knew where to go to find them. When I was working at the office, that's the place I'd go to eat too. Other than that, I was happy with a piece of fruit, or on many days, I met friends at various venues around town.

When it came to dinner, I never quite figured out the custom and practice surrounding evening meals. Not everyone eats dinner, or if dinner is at home, it's eaten late, around 8.00pm and it's a light meal. But when you go out to dinner, or have guests over, then the meal is substantial and has several courses. Especially after a busy day working on the paper, and with no evening arrangements, I'd find myself on the way home at 9.00pm and starving! Unlike the US, grocery stores are not open at that time, and pretty much the only type of take-out you find is at the falafel shops (it's even difficult to find a place to grab a slice of pizza!), so this was my evening meal many a night.

The ingenious concept of *aperitivo* worked very well for me. I often made plans to meet friends around 7:30pm for a glass of wine. Many bars have elaborate complimentary buffets, so that for the €6 it costs for a drink, you could fill up on delicious and substantial food such as at *Colle Beretto* near the Piazza Republica. Another great place for *aperitivo,* no buffet, but with great cheese and meat platters on the menu, is *Le Volpe e l 'Uva* near the Ponte Vecchio. For their view or ambience, other good venues to meet for *aperitivo* (or un caffé earlier in the day) include the roof of the *Continentale Hotel*; the roof of the *Rinasciente Department Store*; *Open Bar*, overlooking the Arno; and the lobbies of both the *Lungarno Hotel* and the *Gallery Art Hotel*.

For either lunch or dinner, or sometimes both, there are so many great places to eat in Florence, it's hard to choose just a handful, but there are a few about which even this non-foodie can get excited. The trick is to look for places outside the tourist center and where the clientele is predominantly Italian.

Semolina, at Sant' Ambrogia, is my favorite neighborhood restaurant with casual, fresh food, at a great price including the best *Spaghetti Carretiere* (pasta with tuna and tomato sauce) I've ever tasted. Tell Adolfo that Nita sent you! *Casalinga* (which means housewife) in Santo Spirito is fabulous for lunch, huge portions of the food traditionally eaten by the Oltrano workers. Don't let the plainly named dishes such as *bollito misto* (a mix of boiled meats in a green sauce) put you off; this is hearty and tasty food.

For that special occasion, very pricey but worth it at least once, head to *Fuor d'acqua;* the seafood is a must and the raw seafood a specialty. Also in the area, *Via Vai* does a wonderful *bistecca fiorentina.* And for *the* best Napolitano pizza, head to *Pizzaiuolo*, in the Sant' Ambrogia area again.

For something different, Austrian royalty, Hapsburg princes no less, will cook for you and serve you at *La Giostra*. This noble family now shares their love of food with us mere subjects in a cozy and friendly restaurant serving great Tuscan *cucina*, enjoyed by Italians and tourists alike. They sneak in a *Weiner schnitzel* and *sacher torte* amongst more obviously Italian goodies including an extensive range of house-made pasta and gnocchi.

At *Sostanza,* locally known *as La Troia,* in Via Porcellina, you'll find great food at *economici* prices and see lots of Italians, even rich ones, always a good sign. The *pollo al burro* is unbelievable. *Troia* means whore, as does, more or less, *Porcellina*. This was once *the* street to pick up a *lady of the night*. A few women, considerably advanced in years, wearing shabby fur coats, still walk the streets in red lipstick and hope. On the same street you'll find *Tredici Gobi* (Thirteen Hunchbacks!) with authentic, good food, well-priced; rigatoni and ribollita are the house classics. And on Via del Moro, *Trattoria Garga,* named for its flamboyant chef-owner Guiliano Gargani is well-known and loved, not least of all for the vibrant artwork adorning the walls, as well the equally colorful presentation of the dishes.

Cibreo, the ristorante, by the Sant' Ambrogio market, is eternally popular, no pasta or grilled meats here, though Fabio Picchi still draws strongly on Tuscan traditions. With no menus available, the waiters pull up a chair and guide you through the options which could include the likes of roasted duck stuffed with minced beef and raisins, or a soufflé of spiced ricotta and potato served with pecorino and ragu. If your budget won't stretch to the main event, for a third of the price for much of the same cuisine, Picchi has a *trattoria* on the same corner. You can try traditional Tuscan soups, slow-cooked braises and if you really want to, a local favorite: *insalata trippa*. It operates on a first-come-first-served basis so you'll need to line up at 7:30pm when it opens for dinner. You'll also find the *Cibreo café,* and *my* barista Isadoro, located in the same area.

Nearby, the deal of the century is, however at Picchi's *Teatro del Sale*. While it's open for breakfast and lunch too, the fixed-price dinner at this unique venue will get you an endless supply of scrumptious food, including wine, coffee and dessert. Entertainment in the comfortable and communal, club-like seating is provided by the frenzy and fire that can be seen through the window into the kitchen; the large and charismatic Picchi theatrically calling away dishes for collection by the waiters; and on-stage, post-dinner performances. The quality of the food usually surpasses that of the acts which sometime include Maria Casi, Picchi's second wife, for whom he created the *Teatro del Sale*.

Quite different, but another must-visit food venue can be found halfway between Florence and Siena in the Chianti countryside at Panzano. *Martica Marcelleria Cecchini* is argued, by many in the know, to be the best butchery in the world, presided over by the larger than life Dario Cecchini. He is a man passionate about all things Tuscan including the cured and fresh meats that he sells in his enchanting shop, along with the likes of his home produced salt and own-recipe mustard, more like a sweet and sour sauce, that tastes scrumptious on anything from cheese to ice cream! A Sunday visit is less *grocery shopping*, and more a celebration of Tuscan life and history. Enjoy the tastings, flowing wine and occasional snatches of Dante recited by Cechinni as he serves his many customers. The party spills out of the shop and onto the ancient streets of Panzano.

Cechinni is the champion of the famous *bistecca fiorentina,* a T-bone steak, traditionally cut from the Chianina or Maremmana breeds of cattle. The steak is grilled over a wood or charcoal fire and then seasoned with salt, black pepper, and olive oil. At a party hosted by *JK Place* (an award-winning boutique hotel), I witnessed the Tuscan butcher make his grand entrance, accompanied by burly bodyguards and holding a violin case handcuffed to his wrist. Opening the case with obvious relish, and to rousing cheers, he revealed the very reason for the party: the return to Florence of the *bistecca fiorentina* after its years in exile as a result of *mad cows' disease*. This drama encapsulated the passion, fun, and complete seriousness, with which the Tuscan's take their heritage - and food.

In case you're wondering what you might drink to accompany all these culinary delights, I know even less about wine than I do about food and am a very occasional drinker. However, if in Florence, you'll be in Chianti country and surrounded by Tuscany's wealth of commercially successful vineyards and prize-winning wines. If you need some advice or an opinion about a wine, vineyard or vintage, anyone and everyone in Italy will be happy to wax poetic about this elixir from the gods and will offer their expertise - whether you solicit it or not!

Leaving and Grieving

Early one morning three months after giving up my apartment in Florence and taking up full-time residence in LA, I'm beginning my daily bike ride along the beautiful Santa Monica ocean front, getting ready to join the other cyclists, joggers and skaters enjoying their morning exercise. To get onto the bike path from my apartment, I have less than a block to ride in the street, which is my excuse for not needing a helmet.

Did I hit the car or did the car hit me? Whatever, I was lying on the street. No pain, which was good. No vision, which was not so good; blood was swimming in my eyes. As I'm not in pain I think I'm okay until I hear one of the people who have rushed over say,

There's blood coming out of the back of her head!

Then I'm frightened.

The ambulance and paramedics arrive. They keep asking me questions,

What year is it? Who's the President? I answer correctly and add,

Let me tell you how totally conscious I am: tell the hospital no one is touching my face until a plastic surgeon has arrived!

Avid *ER* viewing has made me pretty savvy about the things people are likely doing to me now as I lie on the ground. I'm disappointed I can't see the hunks taking care of me, calling me honey, checking my vitals.

So who's the George Clooney of the group? They let me know that pretty boy is the one holding my hand.

I'm scared, I admit; they reassure me that the pool of blood is coming from my broken nose and a gash in my face, not a head injury. At this news, they're all hunks to me.

After a MRI to determine that I don't have any internal derangement (or at least, not any new one), other than the broken nose, I go to another clinic to get fixed by a plastic surgeon. He is recommended to me by Steve who, besides being my fourth grade boyfriend, is a plastic surgeon himself, alas an eye-man not the nose-man I need now. The sunglasses I had been wearing at the time of the collision have slashed into my face so deeply that the bone sticks through, so under the cast they put on when my nose is set, there's a seam of stitches.

The next morning, I awake with two black eyes and a somewhat painful nose. With the cast on my face, I look like a typical middle aged LA woman recovering from a *bit of work.* The good news is that I was extremely lucky that things hadn't turned out very differently; I'd narrowly escaped much worse injuries to my head. The bad news is, that although I'm in a lot of pain and still somewhat in shock and disorientated by the whole experience, no one gives me any sympathy thinking my bandaged look is volunteered for vanity, rather than the result of my recent, unwelcomed trauma.

The accident happened on a Tuesday, and the following few days I begin to get back my equilibrium, physically at least. I also start to examine what is going on in my life. I am self-aware and intuitive enough to know that running into a car on my bike is in some way a symptom of something else going on for me. My 30th birthday car crash on San Francisco Bay Bridge is an earlier example of how such events, thankfully rare, are always a wake-up call, an indication and a bringing to consciousness of something that is festering, unattended, needing focus and action.

Early Saturday morning, I awake with a start: I *don't want my life! This is not the life I want to live!* I don a huge hat and sunglasses and head to synagogue. At the break in the service, very politely, Rabbi Finley averts his eyes as he walks past me. I call out to him,

Rabbi, you need to stop and ask me how I am, this is not the result of an elective procedure, but an accident - I got hit by a car!

He rushes over to comfort me, and I burst into tears; he invites me to his office to talk. I explain,

In the last six months I've given up every dream in my life - all the dreams that I've had for my children - and my own dreams too. I'd hoped that both of my kids would finish their education. The current reality is that my young son is working in a hobby store for practically minimum wage and expecting a child; while my even younger daughter is married, living in a double-wide trailer, high school unfinished.

I cried on his shoulder and continued,

And then there's Florence, I've just given up the most wondrous and extraordinary life that I could ever have imagined living; the international lifestyle that I'd dreamed about experiencing for so long.

When I'd realized I couldn't be away from my new grandson I'd done everything I could to convince my Italian partners that my willingness to travel back and forth several times a year, and my familiarity with technology and using *Skype*, would easily let me continue in the role from afar. But, Italians value the face-to-face connection so much that they just couldn't contemplate this as an option. It was devastating. So now I'd left Florence and *The Florentine and* there was a great big gaping hole in my life.

I tell Rabbi Finley that on top of all this, I feel guilty for being spoiled and sorry for myself,

I shouldn't be complaining at all. My kids are healthy and happy; I have a truly wonderful marriage; I live, if not in Florence, on the ocean, and get to swim, ride my bike and walk on the incredibly beautiful beach every single day.

Not for the first time, and probably not for the last, Rabbi Finley says exactly what I need to hear,

Nita, the things you wanted were good things. For your kids, your life in Italy, you only wanted good things. And before you move on to appreciate what you have now and what they have now, you actually need to grieve the loss: of what you hoped for; expectations not met; your life in Italy. Allow yourself to grieve, to feel sad, and don't judge yourself so harshly because you aren't appreciative of everything right now. And, most importantly, he reminds me: *happiness will return.*

It did.

Too bad I had to break my nose to get the lesson.

Forever Florence

I left Florence in February and didn't return again until September. I didn't quite know what to expect when I went back. Since graduating college, I have lived in three places other than my hometown Detroit and each of them for more than ten years. When I return to visit these places, I'm left with the feeling: *you can never really go back; it just isn't the same.* Some people have gone; others have changed jobs, homes, spouses and phone numbers. Each visit there are fewer friends that I need or want to see or who have time, other than at the weekend, to see me. After two days I don't know quite what to do with myself. My favorite restaurants or stores aren't there anymore. I feel like I am intruding and that I don't belong. I have no life left in these places, everything and everyone, including me, has moved on.

Would I have the same experience in Florence? I was a little worried that people would be too busy to make time to see me, or that the relationships would not be the same, or that I wouldn't have anything to do for the weekend, always one of my biggest challenges in Florence as many people head out to their places in the country and by the sea. I landed with few appointments scheduled, except a *little get-together* a friend had arranged.

Natasha had actually co-ordinated a not so little and very chic *aperitivo* in the yet-to-be-opened Palazzo Tornabuoni. The venue is an elite, luxurious, private members' club and residence in a splendidly restored Renaissance palazzo, very few people in Florence had ever even been inside the long-closed buildings. The decor was lavishly elegant, with the highest of ceilings, tall columns and richly colored furnishings. And there I was, amidst the restoration, entering the one finished *salon* via a grand red-carpeted staircase. The table was laden with the finest foods: prosciutto, salami, parmigiano, bruschetta and bottles of sparkling prosecco, all to be enjoyed with 30 or so of my dearest Florentine friends. Marco laughed,

I wouldn't have expected anything less for you Nita; of course you would return to a party arranged in your honor set in one of Florence's grandest palaces!

That first trip, I ended up spending the weekend with James and Louise Ferragamo in their home by the sea. What with this lovely experience, the amazing aperitivo, seeing other friends and enjoying my daily cappuccino at *Cibreo* once more, it was a fairytale return. I realized I never really *left* Florence.

I now return every four to six months and am fortunate to be able to stay with a friend who has an elegant apartment right on the Arno *due passi* from the Ponte Vecchio, with picture windows (surely the very windows that inspired this name) looking on to the Palazzo Vecchio and the *old bridge*. Stefano, my host, has a bike for me to use when I am there and is always ready to cook me pasta or *pranzo* fresh from the market.

When I visit Florence, the great news is that unlike my previous *going back* experiences in the US, I find that nothing and no one has changed. I get out of the taxi in front of Stefano's apartment, and see my friend Nerina walking by and, before I have brought my bags through the door we've made a date for the next morning. I'm straight into my Florence routine. When I call friends, we set a time for un caffé or dinner over the next few days. Before I hit the pillow that first evening, I feel as if I've never left and it feels great. Still enthralled with Florence's beauty, my spirits soar at the sight of the Ponte Vecchio or at the vision of Il Duomo lit up at night. I attend opening events, dinners and celebrations. Buying a new sweater at Sant' Ambrogio market has never felt so good. I'm back!

Even better, I don't get sad when I leave after just ten days. I'm happy to say I've also fallen in love with my life in Santa Monica: our apartment and its ocean view; the closeness of the beach; the opportunity to swim every day; tons of friends and things to do; loving being near my kids and grandkids; having a ball living like a newlywed with Tony; and working with some brilliant and inspiring clients through my consulting. But I now know that I didn't give up Florence or my life there at all...my *other home* awaits me always and forever.

Florence isn't going anywhere.

Also by Nita Tucker and
available at Amazon.com

*Beyond Cinderella: The Modern
Woman's Guide to Finding a Prince*

How Not to Stay Single

How Not to Stay Single After 40

*How Not to Screw It Up: 10 Steps to
an Extraordinary Relationship*

And look out for:

*Essential Florence: The
Practical Guide to Living in Florence*

Soon available at Amazon.com

To subscribe to *The Florentine* visit:

www.theflorentine.net

Made in the USA
Lexington, KY
04 May 2012